PHENOMENOLOGY AND EDUCATION

VIBS

Volume 68

a volume in
Philosophy of Education
PHED
George David Miller, Editor

PHENOMENOLOGY AND EDUCATION

COSMOLOGY, CO-BEING, AND CORE CURRICULUM

Michael M. Kazanjian

Amsterdam - Atlanta, GA 1998

Cover design by Chris Kok based on a photograph, ©1984 by Robert Ginsberg, of statuary by Gustav Vigeland in the Frogner Park, Oslo, Norway.

∞ The paper on which this book is printed meets the requirements of "ISO 9706:1994, Information and documentation - Paper for documents - Requirements for permanence".

ISBN: 90-420-0330-8

Printed in The Netherlands

DEDICATION

This book is gratefully dedicated to the memory of my grandparents, Kazar and Lucy Dabaghian, and in honor of my mother, Anna Dabaghian.

CONTENTS

EDITORIAL FOREWORD

Shortly before the 1996 presidential election in the United States, the incumbent offered his vision for the future of education. His vision: Hook up every classroom to the Information Superhighway. Immediately, we can dismiss such a proclamation as campaign rhetoric or as the cluelessness of someone out of touch with the "dumbing down" in American schooling. But something more comes out of the incumbent's solution. It suggests that human beings, suffering from educational malnourishment, must be hooked up to the Information Superhighway and fed information intravenously. This vision is also flawed at at a subtle and profound level. It places the machine on one side and the human being on the other instead of recognizing their interdependence.

Michael M. Kazanjian's *Phenomenology and Education* addresses such one-sided visions of the world. Placing himself within the tradition of phenomenology, Kazanjian develops a vision for education in which subject and object are considered to be in a continuum. For phenomenology, phenomena include our experience of relations, values, affections, objects, and mathematical theorems. Subjectivity cannot be reduced to objects, and perception cannot be reduced to sense data.

Kazanjian introduces a phenomenological sense of wholeness into philosophy of education. In the spirit of holism, this text does not merely focus on philosophy of education. The educational sphere is but one of many in a society, interconnected with and slicing through many other spheres. Critiques of urbanization, computers, manufacturing, taxation, and forms of government add dimension to Kazanjian's philosophy of education.

In the initial chapter, three main points emerge: (1) art is the context for the sciences; (2) at the university level, a division of labor between researchers and teachers should be drawn; and (3) a core curriculum revealing our common humanity is to be preferred to distributional requirements. Any sort of specialization (techniques of the sciences) can be holistic only if understood within the context of the arts (meaning, value, cosmic orientation, what it means to be a human being). Kazanjian's proposal for a division of labor in the university is sure to raise more than a few eyebrows. Would having pure researchers and pure teachers prove to increase holism in the university or introduce a dualism that would create two antagonistic classes competing for resources and recognition, each because its limited perspective is unable to grasp the other, one grasping the abstract form, the other the formless content? Without a core curriculum, students easily fall into subjectivism and fail to understand their commonalities as human beings.

Chapters Two through Four discuss production, product design, and automation. Kazanjian's main point is this: Ensure that human beings do not become secondary to production, production design, and automation. Two extremes must be avoided: an insufficient quantity of goods and services versus a pure quantification ignoring the welfare of human beings.

When cultural, psychological, biological, and other contextual factors are taken into account, then a phenomenological position can be secured. The phenomenological position, Kazanjian believes, is the one between the two extremes, resting between solipsism and an objectivism untainted by the human Subject.

In Chapters Five and Six, which address computers and information, Kazanjian objects to the view that computing is simply logic, quantification, rationality, and linearity. Viewed holistically, calculation is understood not only as deliberative, but also predeliberative, occurring within the context of lived history, what Kazanjian calls "Co-Being."

The final two chapters touch on taxation and government. Rejecting both an egalitarian or liberal Rawlsian vision of a state that throws money at problems and a libertarian or Nozickian vision of an anarchic state in which human beings have no legal responsibity to one another, Kazanjian argues for a small, immediate government, what he calls a phenomenological government. A phenomenological government would be run by an elite and would dispense with a Supreme Court.

We cannot throw money or machines (as the incumbent suggested) at problems and expect them to be solved. From a phenomenological perspective, we realize that our objective experience is always subjectively colored. This has a profound impact how we view the most basic issues. Theory cannot be removed from practice; the "I" cannot be separated from the "We"; the abstract cannot be siphoned from the concrete; diversity cannot be separated from commonality; the sciences and arts cannot be divided; machines cannot be viewed apart from the human beings using them; essence cannot be strained from existence; fact cannot be segregated from value; particulars cannot be expunged from universals; the past and future cannot be sifted from the present; and teaching cannot be separated from learning. If this view is correct, then intellectual integrity and a genuinely integrated curriculum go hand-in-hand.

George David Miller
Editor
Philosophy of Education Special Series

ACKNOWLEDGMENTS

While this is an original work, I owe sincere thanks to several people. My long-time friend and colleague, Edmund C. Forst, Jr., Dean of Waubonsee, has suffered, smiled, and triumphed with me in my efforts to develop and bring to fruition this book. His ideas and toil are unseen by all but the author. Ed has read the entire manuscript. Our many conversations, lunches, debates, agreements, and disagreements have made this a better book. He always senses the direction which I tend to miss, and tactfully points toward the correct approach.

My deep appreciation to Robert H. Lichtenbert of Loyola University. He has graciously read and patiently criticized the entire manuscript. His careful eye, perceptive intellect, sense of humor, and ability to read my mind were invaluable toward helping me say what I was trying to say. With his guidance, I can now say this work is precisely the one I wanted to produce.

To say George David Miller has been a special special editor is not redundant. Each page hopefully reflects his intellectual insights, personal interest, and editorial direction. Executive Editor Robert Ginsberg deserves thanks for his advice, and for always putting things into perspective. I appreciate Managing Editor Eric van Broekhuizen's help dealing with the book's mechanics.

I appreciate Jack Johnson, Mary T. Mulcahy, and Kathy S. Killmer who have graciously served as proofreaders.

This acknowledgment would be incomplete without thanks to Sue Arenz for graciously and generously assisting a demanding and impatient author.

The involvement of these individuals, however deep, in no way associates them with any shortcomings in the following pages. The author's refusal to take good advice is the sole reason for those problems.

MMK
Chicago, December 1997

INTRODUCTION

This book introduces the scholarly reader to a phenomenology of education. I start with Descartes's view that subject and object are two distinct substances. This dualism presents a problem that phenomenologists or Continental thinkers resolve. That problem is how to relate dual realities. Phenomenologists assume that intersubjectivity and objectivity are integrated. Subject and object are a continuum. Phenomenologists tell us that to overcome Cartesian dualism and realize the continuum, it is necessary to reintroduce object into subject.

Philosophical literature mentions both pure and applied phenomenology. However, the two types are not mutually exclusive. We may emphasize either pure or applied phenomenology, but are essentially doing phenomenology in each case. Pure phenomenology attempts to resolve the object-subject dichotomy. Yet, a researcher must take into account the social world when speaking of subject and object. Applied phenomenology applies this continuum to social, natural, religious, and other cultural areas. However, to speak of cultural or social applications, we must constantly refer to the subject-object continuum.

My present volume is not about the phenomenological movement. Instead, the following pages show that the subject-object continuum applies as the socio-technological continuum comprising and linking society's institutions. Those institutions underlie and give meaning to work or specialization. Society and technology are a continuum instead of two distinct entities. More accurately, a society that becomes increasingly technical and dehumanized must reintroduce technique into the human dimension, into community or the social context.

I do not speak of the phenomenological movement. But a few words about the origin and meaning of phenomenology will help the reader. Phenomenology is varied. Phenomenologists say different things, and often disagree with each other. However, phenomenologists wish to go "to the things" as "given" in consciousness. The movement evolves from Franz Brentano, and Edmund Husserl's reaction against Cartesian dualism. I start with a few words on Descartes.

Descartes argues that the knowing subject is distinct from the known object. Cartesian dualism means a discontinuity between object and subject. But dualism presents a problem. How can discontinuous substances or realities relate or be continuous? Brentano and Husserl introduce intentionality in order to relate subject and object. Of the two men, Husserl does more extensive work on intentionality. For him, consciousness or subjectivity is not distinct from objects. Intentionality means that subject intends object; the subject is a subject *of* the object. Consciousness is consciousness *of,* and not distinct from the object. We are aware of an object, and not distinct from it.

Husserl's *Ideas Pertaining to a Pure Phenomenology and to a Phenomenological Philosophy*[1] indicates that reduction or bracketing discloses essences, the meaning of objects, and other phenomena. Bracketing suspends our belief in a phenomenon's existence so that we can arrive at the phenomena itself. However, bracketing gives the impression that Husserl is an idealist, or otherwise removed from the world. Later, Husserl writes *Cartesian Meditations*[2] and articulates a more intersubjective and realistic position to demonstrate our connections with objects and people.

Husserl maintains that phenomena are anything that appears or is "given" to consciousness. Phenomena include the experience of relations, values, affection, objects, and mathematical theoroms. This view rejects logical positivism's notion that phenomena is only sensory experience. Rudolf Carnap and Moritz Schlick are dominant logical positivists. For Husserl, phenomenologists are the true positivists because phenomenology posits the original, presuppositionless phenomena.[3] Husserl's student, Martin Heidegger, is another leader in phenomenology, and differs in approach from Husserl.

Heidegger's monumental *Being and Time*[4] says that the question of Being is fundamental to all questions, including the subject-object issue. For Heidegger, subject and object are unified, indeed, all but annihilated, because Being is the pre-reflective, or pre-differentiated unity unfolding through Dasein as our being-in-the-world.[5] Heidegger sees phenomena as the unfolding or opening of Being through Dasein.[6] Our being-in-the-world is a non-differentiated situation, where, Heidegger believes, distinction or calculation can easily lead to misunderstanding of Being as objectified. Heidegger's emphasis on Being opening through our being-in-the-world, and his overly cautious approach to objectification, or calculation, make him seem totally opposed to science and technology. The French phenomenologist, Maurice Merleau-Ponty, does not see such overwhelming prereflection as an answer to unifying subject and object.

Merleau-Ponty is more conciliatory with physiology and the world. His *Phenomenology of Perception*[7] speaks about our being in the world, without emphasizing that a Heideggerian Being unfolds through bodily and perceptual states. Being reveals itself inexhaustibly in our perceptions and existence. However, perceptual experience involves our total and continual existence in the world. Perception is irreducible to the empty and passive subject that only perceives objective sense data. Merleau-Ponty sees perception as the perceiver and the perceived, instead of both being overwhelmed into Being. We can never fully reduce perception to scientific understanding because perception is irreducible to a quantitative reality and methodology. Existence colors our perception. Our total existence shows that we can never pin down the nature of perception, since Being manifests itself as, for example, an object's color, texture, appeal, repulsion, and so forth. We perceive in terms of our existence in the world. Our lived body helps us to be involved in perception and with others. We exist and perceive in the world; the world is not something external to us, but a milieu in which we are constantly engaged with others. Subjects find themselves in a lived world enabling them to be continuous with objects. Merleau-Ponty is more comfortable than Heidegger in believing that idealism and realism ought interact and contribute to each other.

Merleau-Ponty's phenomenology sees persons as spatially and temporally related and relating with each other. Spatially, the world around us is a matrix of subjective-objective interactivity. Temporally, we remember and are connected with the past, and project toward the future.

Finally, Paul Ricoeur systematically brings forth the idea of the subject-object continuum. He does not concentrate on essences and reduction, or on Being as the fundamental question. His *Freedom and Nature: The Voluntary and the Involuntary*[8] says we overcome Cartesian dualism when we reintroduce object into subject.[9] The object is *for* the subject, and subjectivity is *of* the object. Ricoeur's phenomenology deals with psychological, and other day-to-day phenomena, as well as philosophy, as he considers the subject-object continuum in light of human interactions, and behavior.

Ricoeur attempts to maintain good relations with phenomenologists and linguistic analysts. He argues that the subject-object continuum is basically irreducible to analysis of ordinary language, and certainly to any artificial language. However, he believes phenomenologists and linguistic analysts can converse with each other, because analysis concedes a metaphysical reality, and is willing to accept a certain mystery to existence. We must reintroduce reducibility into general irreducibility. Ricoeur's efforts show that we are in the world of persons and objects. A person objectifies within a subjective context. The person must reject subject without objects, and the excarnate object. Objects are subjectively colored, and never excarnate or only external to us. Our physical and physiological existence is colored and oriented through intersubjective contexts that science, linguistic analysis, and artificial language cannot exhaust.

I said Husserl rejects the positivists. Other phenomenologists do the same because positivists deny metaphysics, and attempt to reduce subjectivity to objects, and perception to sense data. Phenomenologists maintain that subjectivity is real, and phenomena are too rich and varied for positivism's completely logical language. From a phenomenological perspective, Carnap and Schlick seriously oversimplify phenomena by trying to reduce existence to objects, and language to completely nonvalue-laden, artificial symbols. In addition, phenomenologists disagree in varying degrees with linguistic analysis, represented by the likes of Bertrand Russell, G. E. Moore, and Ludwig Wittgenstein.

Phenomenologists are often suspicious that linguistic analysis seeks to simplify phenomena more than necessary or possible. From a phenomenological perspective, Russell, Moore, and Wittgenstein go farther than necessary to dissect ordinary language. While analysts do not insist on jettisoning ordinary language with an artificial language, phenomenologists nonetheless see the analysts' approach as generally overly objectifying. Human interactions and phenomena are more mysterious than analysis seems to believe. Phenomenology approaches linguistic analysis cautiously. Husserl and Heidegger are most cautious about linguistic analysis. Ricoeur is relatively comfortable with linguistic analysis. In general, phenomenologists wish to unify subject and object by acknowledging that each is important. Existence means that subjectivity orients objectivity, and that the intuitive orients rationality.

Phenomenologists seek our being in the world as a rational-intuitive whole. They refuse to concede that persons are simply material, scientific, or mathematical entities. Analysis of language cannot totally objectify existence. Phenomenology sees the person as a rich, subjective-objective existence in a world of inexhaustible possibilities and interactions. Philosophy and life cannot be put into a neat mathematical or other symbolic formula. Ordinary language is intricate, and artificial language is too removed from ordinary people. Given the phenomenologists' emphasis on this richness, their rejection of positivism, and their degrees of disagreement with linguistic analysis, we might assume that phenomenology looks mainly to mystery for appreciating existence. But phenomenology also considers objectivity.

In light of this integrative position, phenomenology also disagrees with existentialism. Leading existentialists, such as Albert Camus and Jean-Paul Sartre, are too concerned with the subjective, pre-objective, and pre-calculative. Existentialists see rationalism as almost totally inadequate to deal with existence, so they turn to writing literature. Heidegger is also overly concerned with Being as the irreducible, yet he does not become part of a literary movement. While Sartre uses reason, he also believes that literature is a crucial aspect of life. Existentialism becomes more a literary movement than a rational effort.

Phenomenologists look for a position between extreme objectivity and existentialism's refusal to admit reasonable objectivity. Husserl, Heidegger, Merleau-Ponty, and Ricoeur analyze the subject-object issue in differing intuitive-objective approaches. However, they reject both literature and logic as the keys to understanding existence. Phenomenologists believe literature ignores reasonable objectivity, and that extreme objectivity reduces subject to object.

Phenomenology wants an objectivity *for* subjectivity. Objects are value-laden. A phenomenologist might reflect on history and see the following. Plato wants to unify Heraclitus' change and Parmenides' oneness. Aristotle brings together matter and form. Immanuel Kant attempts to integrate the empirical and rational. Along these integrative lines, phenomenologists are evolving a holistic view which returns objectification into intersubjectivity. Phenomenology's goal is to reintroduce science into art, objective research into intersubjectivity. To use twentieth-century terms, phenomenology attempts to return computation and logic into a mysterious, and holistic human nature. Like the Sabbath, science, including calculation, computers, and intelligent machines, is made *for* humanity. I find it likely that phenomenology, not linguistic analysis, positivism, existentialism, or any other philosophical movement, will bring forth the next Plato, Aristotle, or Kant. The present volume is a humble contribution toward developing an applied phenomenology.

People are *of* objects. Applied, these include cultural institutions and processes. Science, technology, and engineering are part of this general scheme of things. However, in our innovative zeal, let us not ignore the other side of this idea. Objects are *for* people. Institutions and processes, including science, technology, economics, and engineering, are job fields, and work must be *for* society. Phenomenology ought to be our effort to articulate the human-institution continuum. Phenomena are institutions wherein we work. They must be *for* intersubjectivity.

This volume presents the socio-technological nature of eight institutions or themes that I believe are basic to society and work: (1) general education; (2) production; (3) product design; (4) automation; (5) computing; (6) the service or information economy; (7) taxation; and (8) procedure. I argue that general education is the most basic idea. It serves as the framework for the other seven.

This brings me to a point about the American undergraduate. Eventually, college students will face eight issues ranging from general and specialized education to educational, organizational, and political procedures. Each of the eight ideas represents a major issue or question underlying specialization and work. These issues are the following. (1) Why should we study liberal arts? (2) How much ought society produce? (3) Why should engineers be concerned with designing user-friendly products? (4) Can and ought automation replace the worker? (5) Are faster computers possible and ethical? (6) Is the information sector making manufacturing obsolete? (7) How much taxation is necessary? Finally, (8) what are tests, organizations, campaigns, elections, legislation, and constitutionality?

Phenomenological analysis of each institution as socio-technological enables the student to deal with each of these issues. Continental thinking helps the student understand that specialists and scholars within each of the eight are indeed doing phenomenology when they debate and engage in dialogue concerning apparently nonphilosophical, strictly disciplinary themes.

The following pages indicate that humanists and scientists indeed practice the phenomenological approach in apparently nonphilosophical debates. Phenomenology is not just an art. Continental thinking is more than another course. Indeed, philosophy is basic to the arts and sciences and not just another discipline. Thus, phenomenology explores the socio-technological foundations of the humanities and sciences. As such, phenomenology is crucial to the liberal arts and sciences. Phenomenology helps the college student develop a sense of wholeness within each art and sciences, and thus, a wholeness underlying and giving meaning to all areas of work. Continental philosophy reveals the social-technical nature of each institution, disclosing that apparently diverse groups of specialists are, in fact, involved in different forms of phenomenology.

I have organized the eight chapters in this volume to show how disciplinary scholars are, at bottom, doing phenomenology without knowing or acknowledging it. Chapter One is central. It outlines the remaining seven chapters. I point out the generalist-specialist continuum. My world-view is that we must reintroduce specialization into general education if education and work have become overspecialized. Where phenomenologists speak of object *for* subject as a continuum, my fundamental application means the continuum where specialization is *for* general education. Educators arguing for people to be generalists as well as specialists, and especially for the core curriculum, are being phenomenological. Liberal arts indicates the idea of the continuum as general-specialist, and that production-community, product design-user, automation-user, computing-society, information-manufacturing, taxation-society, and procedure-goal are each also a continuum. The remaining seven chapters flesh out this first chapter. I devote a chapter to each of the seven continuums.

Chapter Two defines production as the production-community continuum. We must reintroduce production into community and not allow people to simply produce while destroying neighborhoods and family. Production is *for* community. Many economists point this out. In doing so, they are phenomenological.

Chapter Three reintroduces product design into the user, because a product's design is a design-user-friendly continuum. Design is *for* the user, and not just technology. Engineers who design user-friendly machines, and environments are thereby phenomenological.

Chapter Four tells us that automation is the automation-user continuum. Automation is *for* the user. Mechanical motion ought not, and often cannot, occur alone, according to many engineers. In saying this, they are reintroducing automation into the worker, and talking phenomenologically.

Chapter Five reintroduces computing into society, because philosophers and nonphilosophers alike argue that computing is the computing-society continuum. Computing is *for* the social. Computer scientists speaking this way are revealing phenomenological validity. They reintroduce computing into the social.

Chapter Six shows that information is the information-manufacturing continuum. Information or the service sector is *for* manufacturing. Economists who argue for this integration are thereby phenomenological. We reintroduce information into manufacturing.

Chapter Seven points out the tax-society continuum. Taxes are *for* society, and never may be only raised or lowered. Taxation is, at bottom, philosophical, and, indeed, phenomenological. We must reintroduce taxes into society.

Finally, Chapter Eight reveals the procedure-goal continuum. Procedure is *for* social goals. Campaigns, elections, legislation, constitutionality, and the notion of three branches of government are basically phenomenological and not strictly political issues. We reintroduce campaigns into elections, and legislation into constitutionality.

My volume, then, attempts to show to the scholarly reader that philosophy, especially phenomenology, is something most specialists are indeed doing. It is basic to knowledge and life. It is fundamental to the arts and sciences. Phenomenology is fundamental to work.

ONE

SPECIALIZATION *FOR* GENERAL EDUCATION

From a phenomenological perspective, cosmology is the most general statement about a nation's economic and national well-being. In that spirit, my present chapter outlines this book's remaining chapters. The phenomenological method links a theory of existence with economics and productivity. Whereas economists see the Gross Domestic Product (GDP) as an index of the nation's economic strength, and often its general health as well, those who consider how much the nation is producing must primarily think about society's belief concerning people and nature. A productive nation produces a beneficial, holistic theory of existence, instead of only a quantitative equation assuming the human and natural to be purely physical entities. Humanity and nature are irreducible to mathematics and physics. Higher amounts of goods and services (including more and more books and research into cosmology) are of no value if society assumes that humans beings and nature are no more than the result of subatomic forces and particles. More important than working, having a job, or producing increasingly higher GDP are the meanings and values about human nature, purpose, and destiny underlying physics and math.

In this chapter, I argue that the healthy nation sees a theory of existence to be a general education or liberal arts and sciences, especially in terms of a . National and economic well-being are served primarily when workers examine themselves as persons and consider the meanings and values underlying jobs. Each person is a person as the context for worker, and is not explainable solely in terms of physics and mathematics. This requires that I begin with an analysis of the phenomena that a cosmology explains.

Cartesian dualism views subject and object as two distinct substances. In this book, subject and object become an ethical issue. Objects are goods and services. Higher quantities of objects mean little when seen in isolation from intersubjectivity, goals, meanings, purposes. Just as objects are objects only *for* subjectivity, and subjectivity is subjectivity *of* the object, so the quantity of goods and services must be only *for* people, and people are only *of* goods and services. A cosmology is the most general good, expressing a society's beliefs. A nation does a disservice to itself if it sees national well-being as the sum of objects while it assumes that phenomena to be explained are only physical bodies in space, and subatomic particles, and forces. Phenomena are jobs or objects *for* people as generalists. Generalists believe in an intersubjective theory of existence of jobs.

1. Work Is Irreducible to Physics

Astrophysicists argue that the phenomena to explain or incorporate into a single conceptual framework are astronomical, atomic, and subatomic matter. This approach manifests the thoroughly scientific, quantitative approach. The heavens put on an awesome display, inspiring both the romantic and the intellectual. Lovers speak of the silvery moon, scientists of the stars, galaxies, space, and time. How many millions acknowledge astrology? Additionally, while the subatomic world is invisible, philosophers, mystics, and others have expended no little time attempting to determine basic elements constituting our unseen physical surroundings. The effort to find the meaning of existence has come to denote a rational, experimental, quantitative inquiry into the largest astronomical, and smallest subatomic domains. But let us look more closely at this issue.

Students and adult workers need cultural, social, and philosophical foundations for professional skills and productivity. Experts in adult education refer to the importance of cultural knowledge basic to specialization, work skills, and technology. Judy Fauri[1] points out that language, literature, history, culture, and empathy are foundations upon which to build specific job skills. These topics give meaning and perspective to work. The phenomenologist can be comfortable with these views. Social phenomenologist Alfred Schutz[2] indicates that social, economic, and cultural institutions are the context in which we are born and gain our identity. Putting Schutz's ideas in disciplinary terms that a modern academician would understand, lived history consists of moral codes, economic situations, religion, language, art, education, and philosophy. Whereas, while astrophysicists may believe art and science are reducible to physical laws, phenomenologists say lived history, the liberal arts, humanities, and science are relatively autonomous and therefore irreducible to physics. A cosmology would have to take into account the reality of art and science.

The physical universe or world outside is real. No one except the ultimate skeptic or solipsist can doubt that astronomy and astrophysics talk about something real. However, that sentence says more than we think. If the scientist, or, more accurately, the astrophysicist, cosmological physicist, and astronomer are producing information about the physical world, the physical phenomena that they wish to explain are more than an independent reality detached from these scientists' behavior. Professional researchers, by working, provide us with data and theory concerning physical phenomena. Physics is a human activity, profession, or field of work informing society about one aspect of existence. Physicists know that other jobs exists, from the mostly manual to the highly theoretical. Each job deals with other types of phenomena.

Physics produces goods and services involving knowledge of the physical universe. We cannot isolate economics from anything, including physics. Ask any physicist wishing to work on the superconducting supercollider (SSC) about politics and economics. You soon see that physics is a job, and there are other jobs, such as those of government officials, capable of providing or funding for the SSC. These officials deal with the phenomena of laws, funding, and national priorities. The nation includes carpenters, police, doctors, clergy, cabdrivers, the military. Each of these work with their set of phenomena: wood work, crime, illness, spirituality and human life, transportation, a nation's external enemies.

Jerome B. Weisner says humanists must study and not ignore science, and scientists should understand and not avoid the humanities.[3] Additionally, things are both measurable and immeasurable. For Arthur D. Hall, there are degrees of quantification whereby numbers hold varying significance.[4]

The ultimate phenomena that human beings must explain are not just the stars, galaxies, and constituents of atoms. Because physical phenomena are something about which we hear thanks to the working physicist, then the primary phenomena to explain are the fields of work as such. Increasing production does little if people do not put the fields into meaningful perspective, consider values, and appreciate human life in its historical, theological, philosophical, and cultural foundations. This chapter does not, indeed cannot, detail such foundations; its aim is only to outline their importance in a cosmology and GDP, and argue their irreducibility to science, and astrophysics.

2. Cosmology Is Irreducible to Physics

If, as I argue, physical phenomena are at least secondary to the most general phenomena of work, then the foundations of work can be approached through the general work of general education. Without the behavior of human beings working to develop knowledge of physical or other phenomena, the behavior of stars, galaxies, and atom or of any particular human being cannot become known and codified. Additionally, if general education is to explain the areas of work as the fundamental phenomena, it follows that a theory of existence is what society calls general education, the liberal arts and sciences. Phenomenological cosmology, then, takes the holistic approach to such a theory, instead of falling into a totally quantitative field that is only one among the arts and sciences. Cosmology is cultural, the foundations of work and the nature of the person, and is not a mathematical equation concerning physical forces and entities.

From the perspective of Co-Being, humanity needs to explain what people do, instead of only what physical forces, particles, and bodies do. Workers, specifically physicists, are doing some things that inform us of what the physical forces and particles are doing. To understand or explain the physical universe, we must begin by probing and appreciating human behavior, meaning, and values, because physicists are people and physics emerges from the social context. In that case, explaining meanings and values underlying special fields is more important than exploring and putting into perspective the activities of any one field, including physics.

Meanings and values are crucial to the phenomenological approach to cosmology. Phenomenologists point out that meanings and values determine how individuals deal with their environments. People do not just react to surroundings. People behave in ways that express their basic ideas, convictions, or beliefs. Few of us do things because we are technically able to do them. General education advocates are phenomenological in that they promote a liberal arts curriculum, giving meaning, value, and order—cosmos—to specialization. Specialties cannot give meaning to themselves. General education is irreducible to the sum of specialties. Ernest L. Boyer's foreword to Nell P. Eurich's *Corporate Classrooms*[5] advises that liberal arts provide the meaning, values, and context within which job skills make sense. Liberal arts and sciences is the cosmos or order within which specialization gains its meanings, values, and orientation.

Liberal arts and science does two things. First, it generates and provides meaning or context for the kind and number of arts and sciences jobs. Second, it determines how art orients science within each job.

Ironically, Boyer's thoughts concern the importance of liberal arts for continuing or adult education, and are not directed specifically toward the undergraduate experience. Is general education's role of meaning and values for specialization emerging from the adult world of work instead of the college level? This may well be, since adults believe they need only work or produce, and educators now find that work skills and technique are only part of any profession: meaning and liberal arts values constitute the core of jobs. Hopefully, this integrating attitude will trickle down to the college and university levels, admonishing the student that a major field of study requires a cosmos of general education.

Meaning involves lived history, the arts and sciences as previously mentioned. Jobs themselves as arts and sciences, not just the physical world, need to be put into perspective. But jobs or fields of work as arts and sciences are structurally different from general education which attempts to educate the worker in the liberal arts.

Strictly speaking, this means there may be two kinds of lived history. Jobs themselves categorize lived history as various arts or humanities and science: economics, art, language, philosophy, education, business, and others. This means art and science. But the liberal arts show that and how humanities orient the sciences as such. The liberal arts are not just a listing of lived history, but show how its humanities orient its science. Richard Bellman and Albert Einstein have pointed out that art orients science, or art is science's context.[6]

I argue that this demonstrates a link between phenomenology, especially applied phenomenology, cosmology, and education. Lived history, considered carefully and integratively, comprises the cosmology or social context underlying production and specialization. Society benefits from the high GDP when work is seen in the context of culture, and human beings and workers are considered as persons instead of only technicians. Phenomenological cosmology means general education is our cultural or social involvement in understanding, developing, and refining specialization. Specialization is irreducible to production and technical know-how. It requires meaning, values, orientation or cosmos for the worker to be first of all a human being. People as culture determine available jobs; people as culture help define ethical and unethical behavior and work.

Cosmology as general education is the embodiment of specialization. Modern thinking on departmentalization has emptied the liberal arts cosmos of its specialized fields, just as Cartesian dualism emptied object from subjectivity. Where Ricoeur[7] says we must reintroduce the object into subject or intersubjectivity, so cosmology regains its holistic status only when the phenomenologist and phenomenological education reintroduce specialization into liberal arts and sciences. If objects are incarnate or embodied, all disciplines are meaningful and incarnate only within general education. General education and specialization are not two kinds of learning, with cosmology often associated only with the physical and mathematical specialties. Cosmology is the general orienting the special. Cosmology is our cultural and intellectual involvement with specialization.

Phenomenologically, general education is general education *of* specialization, just as subject is subject *of* the object. Conversely, specialization of human work is specialization *for* general education, just as any object is an object *for* subjectivity or intersubjectivity. Sensory deprivation experiments have shown no subject exists without object. No experiment shows that general and special education are connected. Perhaps history, civilization, phenomenology, and phenomenologically oriented specialists in education and other fields provide us with such assurance.

If specialization means jobs outside the typical academic framework, general learning occurs in the university setting. A university is the ultimate universe or unity, revealing the taxonomy underlying all areas of work. Cosmology would be more than a department within a university as some scholars suggest, though I am pleased with their willingness to bestow departmental status on cosmology. Cosmology would be the university itself, with general education the university's main goal. With this in mind, the university does two things.

First, the academic world acts as a think tank where professional intellectuals never teach the undergraduate, and perhaps never the graduate student. The professionals may teach each other. Their role here is to develop knowledge, research, publish; that is, they would bring about and constantly refine a cosmology. Professional intellectuals become links between society and government by advising and helping officials see the best things to legislate. In this sense, the think tank employs the cosmologist whose main task is to clarify and perpetuate tradition.

Second, the university as an academic community ought to act as a place where teachers or professors educate students beginning at the undergraduate and proceeding to the graduate level. Here, the professional would never be required to publish. In this sense, the cosmologist is one who perpetuates tradition by helping students understand and appreciate it. Yet, the cosmologist does not just transfer tradition.

Should our heritage need improvement and necessary change, the cosmologist is responsible for modifying the past so that teacher, researcher, and student learn something more meaningful. Teaching the undergraduate and graduate is the main goal of academia. The university combines under one roof the think tank, where research and development occur, and academia, in which teaching and learning occur. Publishing is the purpose of the think tank; teaching is that of academia.

This is not a dichotomy. It is a division of labor. People who want to teach and have little or no interest in writing should not perish if they do not publish. Those who wish to publish and have no desire to teach may then do so without being forced to enter the classroom. Scholars who wish to teach and publish, may do both. If we force all teachers to publish, the quality of publication can decline, and only the quantity increases.

The think tank develops and refines general education or the theory of existence, which academics then convey to the students. What of intellectuals who enjoy both publishing and teaching? This poses no great problem. We must always have room for professionals who may wish to divide time between the two university aspects, spending several years in each area.

Ironically, public and media become excited over books portraying cosmology as an astrophysical field, while so many students and others continually ask the value of liberal arts over more practical education. The enthusiasm with which society greets advances in scientific cosmology suggests that deep inside, people have the need for studying order. This enthusiasm might be an Occidental prejudice having begun with the Greek interest in cosmos as order. However, ideas are not wrong just because they originate in the West. Order can be a Western contribution to civilization. Is it conceivable that the university has neglected to organize and market the proper cultural or phenomenological view of order or cosmology as Co-Being? Departmentalization of knowledge is not orderliness, coherence, or perspective.

Departmentalization within the university, and emphasis on jobs outside, are like a Cartesian view: "I work, therefore I am a human being." Phenomenologists would say *cogito ut sum* instead of *cogito ergo sum*. Similarly, they would say "I work as a person," instead of "I work therefore I am a human being." Liberal arts purists are also wrong when they argue that "I am cultural, therefore I work or produce by creating ideas." Phenomenological cosmology would mean that I work within the cultural context of refining job technique, caring for people, taking civilization and institutions into account, and thereby producing as a social or communal individual. I work in terms of the meanings, beliefs, and assumptions that society and I entertain about work. Co-Being asks that we not empty our cultural nature or communal constraints of production, making specialization an end in itself. Work is *for* the person, the person is a person *of* productivity. This may have a Kantian root in that work means we must care, and produce adequate goods and services for others.

Intersubjective cosmology, therefore, raises to the highest level of generalization quantum theory's notion that the physical observer influences the particle's measurements. Where relativity theory sees scientists more or less detached in observing large astronomical bodies moving with predictable motions and positions, quantum theory has shown that we cannot just stand back, observe, and predict subatomic particles. In quantum theory, the person's act of measuring particles influences those measurements. Stars, galaxies, and other large bodies may be external, as it were, free of our measuring methods, but subatomic particles are measured only in terms of our influence upon the measurements. Likewise, this physical phenomena is someone's job, and each job is influenced by social, cultural, and personal values. No area of work is totally external to the human being. We have to consider a society, its institutions, values, and goals in order to account for or explain what kinds of jobs people do. Thus, a cosmology is irreducible to the four forces: weak, strong, gravitational, and electromagnetic. Important as these may be within astrophysics, they are the product, the goods and services, of a particle field of human behavior. If the most general form of phenomena are jobs, and astrophysics or physics is one among all professions, then humanity and nature are irreducible to astrophysical laws. National productivity suffers in the long term when scientists can convince themselves, their nonscience colleagues, and the government that phenomena are basically physical and that a unified field theory is nothing more than mathematical equations uniting weak, strong, electromagnetic, and gravitational forces. That myoptic, scientistic instead of scientific view implies that astrophysics has more implications for theological, and philosophical questions than the reverse.

Should something like the superconducting supercollider be built? What of the space station? Applied phenomenologists might agree, depending on budgetary situations, but argue that these activities should not be the cornerstone of knowledge and a theory of existence. Physical knowledge is part of science and therefore only part of the arts and sciences, only a portion of jobs and work. We do not need a great crash program to find a physical field theory. We do not need a Manhattan Project for such a search. Co-Being is the position that humanity and nature are fundamentally irreducible to subatomic realities. Astrophysical truths give us only a small portion of the broader knowledge we need.

Scientists, even astrophysicists, are not a monolith. Some believe existence is basically numeric and that in time we will discern all the quantitative laws necessary to understand and predict. However, other astrophysicists disagree. They share with many phenomenologists the belief that the universe consists of something irreducible. Be this supernatural, physical but holistic, or perhaps a reality of which we presently know or imagine nothing, some scientists concede that there are more things in heaven and earth than Horatio dreams of. Many scientists cannot even envision experiments to prove or disprove certain current proposals.

Astrophysics plays an important role in cosmology because it contributes to knowledge of the external world. However, astrophysics is not the fundamental theory of existence. Whatever astrophysics learns of the physical universe, the humanities informs us of our wonder and awe that we as human beings are capable of learning that knowledge. The fundamental field theory is not astrophysical, but humanistically oriented science including astrophysics. We should never ignore how and that people came to originate the idea of the origins of the physical world.

An interesting aside concerns the quark. Scientists often retain or reject a theory depending on experiments. Quark theory tells us that the proton is reducible to the quark, but no experiment thus far has been able to liberate the quark from the proton. Some experiments imply that modifications in instrument construction can bring success, for the proton may break apart in ways strange to us now. Science cannot verify an object unless experiments prove it exists in isolation. So one might think quark theory would be discarded. However, so powerful is its ability to explain, that it remains.

How do we accept a theoretically real, experimentally unverified object? Physics sees a problem, phenomenology does not. A few physicists suggest that nature is trying to tell us the quark exists, but only represents an irreducible entity. We cannot cut the proton further. From a phenomenological perspective, this can easily mean that the proton consists of co-objects or co-particles incapable of liberation. The quark may be a complex, whereby the object is really an interrelated series of objects or forces. It has parts, but these constitute each other, and neither aspect can be broken from the others. Hence, astrophysics may have come to the end of the road of a nature in which breaking down physical reality is limited. Astrophysics cannot explain physical reality by liberating and exhibiting an isolated thing called the quark. Quark theory may well mean a complex, more theoretical than experimental notion where quantum theory reaches its logical conclusion. Relativity theory says we are detached observers of stars and planets; quantum theory says the individual is attached to measurements of subatomicity; and quark theory may mean that explanation involves theory and coping, and not just experiments, because objects themselves are involved with each other.

Indeed, astrophysical laws are unable to explain even the sciences as such. Chemistry and biology exhibit unique and relative autonomy to be considered part of astrophysics. Chemical and biological activity cannot be completely predicted. Uncertainty is always with us, if only because people are involved in their prediction.

How unique is humanity? The arts, humanities, and social fields other than natural science appear to show more fundamental irreducibility. Scholars may be able to interpret, understand, appreciate, or wonder, but they cannot always exactly predict or manipulate what human society does. Some scientists and scientifically oriented humanists argue that improved quantitative methods and knowledge can help accelerate our efforts to predict, to reduce knowledge to mathematics and physics. However, it is important to see that the human being is doing this, and the issue arises as to how much prejudice is involved in such predictions. Moreover, if, as seems clear, people use less than six percent of their brains, would increased mental capacity mean only quantitative ability, or is there more? Would a more evolved species result in a human nature more inclined to love, appreciate, wonder, and feel awe than simply assume the world and humanity are objects? It appears that the more we probe life, the more we see the importance of wonder as well as analysis.

A phenomenological field theory to explain existence therefore unites human disciplines, of which physics with its relativity and quantum theories is only one. Additionally, intersubjectivity and the holistic attitude suggest that wonder is the subcontext for scientific probing as such, within the basic context of liberal arts and sciences underlying job phenomena. Bringing together relativity and quantum theories still gives us only science, indeed, only physics. There remain at least chemistry and biology. But when liberal arts and sciences bring together all jobs within the cultural context, we can more fully and deeply explain human behavior and production, including the need to produce a field theory, whether in physics or more generally. Indeed, with liberal arts and sciences, society explains, but also wonders and appreciates, that jobs, nature, and humanity simply *are*.

Wonder and analysis, whether philosophical or art and science, are both vital. This integration raises a question of the search for the next Heidegger. True, Heidegger has made an impact on philosophy, theology, and knowledge in general through his efforts to secure a place for wonder, holism, and irreducibility. However, Wittgenstein displayed a shift from analysis to wholeness, and therefore may be considered to have contributed to the broader, intersubjective context. Is it important to search for the next Heidegger or Wittgenstein? If integrating whole and part are vital, the next thinker is probably heir to Wittgenstein. But given Heidegger's impact, the next thinker also inherits Heidegger. Is that person therefore the next Heidegger and Wittgenstein? That seems overly cumbersome. Why not consider the next Heidegger as the greatest living philosopher? To date, Ricoeur appears to be a strong contender as Heidegger's successor. I argue that Ricoeur ought to be the next great thinker, following Wittgenstein and Heidegger. Ricoeur has done well in proposing that Cartesian dualism can be resolved best through an intersubjectivity where we reintroduce objects into subjectivity: objects are *for* subjectivity, subjects are only *of* objects. This integration of objectivity and intersubjectivity brings us to an interesting twist on cosmology.

If we restrict cosmology to religion and physics, the issue of creation emerges. That question cannot be dismissed. But the broader question is more than who or what created the universe, where did nature originate, and so forth. Religious, physics, and related professionals are asking these questions. Laypersons also inquire, regardless of their jobs. But we look to the professionals to enlighten us with their insights. Again, professionals posing and contributing to this question are doing so as they work and produce. I suggest that more general than the issues of the physical world's origins may well be our values and goals generating the jobs and questions that particular fields ask. If, as phenomenologists argue, work expresses our meanings, values, and goals and is not just a reaction to the external environment, then irreducibility, involvement and wholeness are fundamental to a theory of existence. People are not just physical entities. Part of the liberal arts and science is the humanistic position that, while science and language analysis help free us from a metaphysical and humanistic morass, the metaphysical and human are irreducible to quantification and verification. Science and cognitive clarity are important, but the human, nonnumeric, or holistic is the context for analysis with which we must learn to cope. It does us little good to produce more and more, while reducing knowledge and life to astrophysics, attempting total prediction and cold numbers.

3. General Education Is Cosmology

Even if cosmology is general education orienting specialization and is irreducible to astrophysics, what method is best for conveying the liberal arts and sciences to the student? What benefit comes to society with high GDP if students learn general education in a fragmented, purely quantitative method of courses offered in the cafeteria fashion? The sum total of courses, chosen almost totally by the student's individual preference, cannot constitute a liberating experience. The student needs liberation not only from excarnate technique and work, but also from his or her own subjectivism. Intersubjectivity or Co-Being triumphs.

The search of physics for a quantitative rather than a mythological theory of existence is interesting. Astrophysicists argue that ancient mythologies offer inadequate cosmologies because each is based on the particular culture's theological, social, mystical biases instead of rational, intellectual investigation. Intellectual inquiry is intersubjective. It takes into account a more uniform theory of existence with which individuals in all enlightened cultures can concur and that all understand. People are social; they are a common link and part of the past, present, and future. Both astrophysics and phenomenology share the basic notion that individuals are one, united from the earliest point in the past to the farthest we can imagine in the future. The future is more than a serial progression, a succession of events from the the past and present. Tomorrow is not just another, distinct time from today. It perpetuates common goals, values, and meanings where tomorrow's people look upon us as having generated and helped shaped them.

To be the same from the past, present, and future means that they ought to share a common view of the universe, of life. Given this need for a uniform theory of existence, a core curriculum is better than the distributional requirements. The core consists of the same content for every student. Of course, where the astrophysicist would insist on the scientific dimension, the liberal arts and sciences can give a humanistic-scientific core: intellectual uniformity cannot imply a purely quantitative world view. Unity is unity instead of diversity, but not the quantitative isolated from the nonquantitative.

The distributional requirements have a serious flaw. Phenomenology calls it subjectivism. Subjectivism is not intersubjectivity; it is being alone, or solipsism, as opposed to Co-Being. The ancient communities with their theological, mystical cosmologies have something we do not in the distributional requirement program. A given ancient society socializes its members to share in its world view. Each member believes in the same theory of existence. Astrophysicists and anthropologists point out that these theories differ from culture to culture and are therefore not uniform, but a phenomenologist would note that at least every member of a tribe believes in a common view. Students in a distributional requirement program certainly cannot be said to share a common curriculum. Whereas members of a tribe share the same cosmology, while tribal cosmologies themselves differ, students in a distributional requirement program do not share even a university's view. Without a core curriculum, university students do not share a view reflecting the school. That school's defense seems a contemporary one.

Ancient tribes strive for social cohesion. Each culture may differ from other cultures and each may generate a different cosmology, but at the very least members within each share a common theory of the universe. A college or university is not a local tribe, community, or social unit. Although its members may see themselves as part of a common bond, that bond is not a cohesive unity that members may not leave at will. The tribe is a social unity, with a single cultural framework. The college can be multicultural, and its students come there for personal and intellectual development, for jobs. A tribe's members are born and raised there, in general. A college's students and faculty are recruited. During their studies, many students in fact go on field trips to other schools and countries, and after graduation most do not continue living in the area of the campus. But this does not justify denying the validity of a core curriculum.

Human beings are human, regardless of their cultures. Multiculturalism seems to fail in that it perceives particular cultures as such, without seeing the transcultural notions of intersubjectivity, institutions, meanings, and values. However diverse their students and faculty, colleges and their curricula must be more than multicultural. A core curriculum admits that people are social, intersubjective, Co-Being whatever their gender, ethnicity, or religion. They have common questions of general and specialized learning, of art and science, of meaning and work, of being human and a worker. Colleges also have the common issue of debating the core curriculum and distributional requirements. The distributional requirement program is grounded in subjectivism, with students dreaming up their own views as if alone. The core helps students see themselves as Co-Being, the same regardless of national origins, religion, or sex. The distributional requirement program characterizes people as temporally and spatially isolated, almost solipsistic, which human beings are not. However, the core curriculum argues that individuals are temporally and spatially Co-Being: the same here and there, the same yesterday, today, and tomorrow.

Thus, a nation's well-being suffers with high productivity when students are encouraged to deny a common intellectual cosmology. Knowledge is not only reduced to astrophysics (if that is possible), but method is reduced to subjectivistic choice (very possible). If an ancient tribe wishes to inculcate its members with a common sense of being one genealogical family and having a single world view, the core curriculum wishes to instill students from diverse backgrounds with a common, intersubjective theory of existence regardless of cultural diversity. For example, we cannot argue that racism and sexism are wrong, that people of all races, creeds, and colors are human beings, and then argue that individualism and the student's own choice for courses is the only alternative for learning liberal arts. If races, creeds, colors, and religions are based on a common humanity, dignity, and respect for the person as person, this does not mean we allow the individuals to be only themselves. It means something deeper: diversity reveals a human, cross-cultural unity we should acknowledge as more important than the diversity.

The distributional requirement program implies a subjectivism with possible serious consequences. A logical conclusion of permitting or encouraging students to "do their own thing" leads to divisiveness in a nation of adults. Such divisiveness individual and certain group tastes are put above national cohesion. If, for example, schools tolerate subjectivistic curricula, will this result in society's accepting and even encouraging subjectivistic morality, ethics, and language? If academia puts high value and meaning on students pursuing their own personal interests and capabilities, a nation can eventually spend unnecessary time debating over which language is official, and, indeed, whether there ought to be an official national language.

What has occurred in the former Soviet Union could be a harbinger for any nation in which freedom of speech and personal choice go too far. Students come to higher education to learn to think and become reflective individuals instead of passive observers of external rules, and technique. Yet the individuals who forget their roots, social responsibilities, national cohesion, and a certain sense of basic stability among nations of the world falls into a subtle solipsism. Students may read many books, listen to lectures, and never deny other people or the external world, but are learning only to reinforce their own personalities, biases, motivations, and interests at the expense of their Co-Being.

Society cannot have it both ways. It cannot, for example, maintain that we legislate and impose laws forbidding racial discrimination, and then go along with the distributional requirement program, one axiom of which is to allow students to develop according to their own interests and abilities. Their interests may be unethical, shortsighted, unenlightened, illegal, or at least incomplete. Does the school then permit them to hate? We hope the school is more sophisticated than permitting hate. Their abilities may be embryonic. Does the college permit them to learn humanities and ignore science, or the reverse, if the students have come from a background deficient in one or the other? That is not a college's aim. Universities must help the students develop and fulfill themselves as total persons with maturing interests and abilities. Students should learn a holistic and intersubjective instead of subjectivistic theory of existence.

Every student is part of previous generations and passes values and meanings on to future humanity. Intersubjectivity in method denies the validity of distributional requirement program's subjectivism. Such a method also rejects a methodological objectivism in which the university would require students to listen and never ask, inquire, or demand self-respect. A core curriculum rejects the notion that students should develop only their own ideas of existence, because all people are interrelated as Co-Being. It also rejects the notion that students only observe and take notes without necessary questions, especially if they do not understand something. The distributional requirement program is more fragmented than an ancient society's superstitions, because no such culture allows individuals to imagine their own personal mythology.

Methodological intersubjectivity means we reintroduce institutinal requirements into the student's identity as Co-Being. Thus, the college does not ignore the individual's abilities and interests or the school's needs. Typical students will look at their abilities and interests within the social and intersubjective context of humanity's nature. Interests harmful to them and others ought to be understood, eliminated, or otherwise modified and better ones developed. Our capabilities will be fostered to the extent that we benefit ourselves as persons and humanity. Methodological subject and object come together in the well-developed core curriculum.

The core curriculum is never automatically intersubjective in terms of content. Just as astrophysics demanding cosmological uniformity might insist on a quantitative core, so humanists can go to the other extreme, teaching the same humanities to students while ignoring science. Co-Being in content unifies science and art by showing the humanities as science's context, not just another field. If, as I argue, general education underlies and gives meaning to disciplines or job fields, liberal arts and sciences have to be humanistically oriented science, and neither a subjectivistic humanism nor objectivistic science.

National well-being and productivity are helped fundamentally when students coming to college see their personality in light of intersubjective contexts. Productive graduates produce, choose, respect themselves, gain knowledge and perspective in terms of social institutions, cultural values, and a broad spectrum of the human experience. Tomorrow's worker will acknowledge cultural differences, but be able to do this properly by sensing that ever so subtle, all too elusive orientation that all humans need belongingness, care, self-respect, festivity, heroes: in a word, the context of lived history.

This is not to deny that college and graduate students think only in dry, cold cross-cultural themes. No honest core curriculum can extricate itself from historical themes, personalities, or an outline of cultural diversity. But familiarizing students with diversity does not mean permitting them to study what and how they wish. Moreover, a core curriculum valid for one institution is therefore valid for every other school.

A Harvard University faculty member has stated that that college's core cannot be a model for other universities. The professor argued that different traditions and finances mean that other colleges need to develop their own cores. However, this is wrong. The core of knowledge does not mean a core at only one place and time. Scientists do not develop theories and perform experiments to be valid at only one time and place. A truth found or conclusion reached at MIT applies as well to CalTech, Podunk, Moscow, or Beijing Universities, or a theological seminary teaching about that topic. For that faculty member to deny that a core ought to be a model is akin to what scares the astrophysicist who denies the adequacy of ancient cosmologies because they are provincial. Identifying a university's core curriculum with the academic institution developing it and indicating that we go no further in showing it is for others, is like each ancient tribe having its own cosmology.

Presumably, an American university's core curriculum is written in English. That curriculum consists of ideas, arguments, and other aspects intelligible, acceptable, and reasonable for any school In America. For that matter, it may present few problems to foreign colleges and universities. This curriculum is based on reasonable, rational inquiry, debate, scholarship, and professionalism instead of mysticism, divine revelation, and local traditions. Therefore, faculty members who say it is only for their college fail to realize humanity's intersubjective, social nature linking past, present, and future. These faculties are no more sophisticated than the ancient tribe that develops its own myth as different from other tribes.

A core curriculum acknowledging the intersubjectivity of all students on campus past, present, and future must also acknowledge the Co-Being of all students in all colleges everywhere. When professors in other colleges seek information from a prestigious university's core curriculum, they display the instinct that all people are Co-Being, interrelated, and seek the unity that comprises humanity.

Local mythologies or cosmologies are due to imagination, superstition, and similar methods other than intellectual inquiry and scholarship. Co-Being shows us that a cosmology as core curriculum frees knowledge from spatio-temporal restrictions. What is core is valid anywhere, anytime. To say one college's core cannot and should not be a model for others, to say one school's core is to be different from that of others, is to fall into the "primitive's" trap. It means people on different campuses are not looking at the same reality; are institutionally solipsistic or subjectivistic; and cannot share the common view. Imagine a scientist finding an experimental discovery, even theoretical breakthrough, but insisting that this is only that scientist's interpretation and not reality for all.

4. Conclusion

The most general sense of national economic and general health involves production of goods and services (objectivity) for a general (intersubjective) theory of the universe. Jobs are the basic phenomena to be understood and appreciated in terms of a core curriculum. That core manifests lived history as past, present, and future. To produce more and more goods and services is wrong when a nation considers phenomena as only those contained in physics and tries to reduce people and nature to astrophysical laws.

The distributional requirements are subjectivistic instead of intersubjective, but the core curriculum option in general education is correct, because it shows humanity's Co-Being as students learn about their past, present, and future: individuals as social. Students are part of the same world, and to permit undergraduates to select *their* own general curriculum means the college is telling students that the world is *their* own instead of social or ours.

Phenomenological cosmology rejects excarnating quantitative order from cultural contexts; Co-Being reintroduces quantitative order or cosmos into intersubjectivity. Order is an intellectual construct and not just scientific as astrophysics implies. Ultimately, order, cosmos, means the human being's effort to discern meaning in human phenomena, because humanity underlies what it perceives as phenomena. Phenomena are what people see as phenomena.

TWO

PRODUCTION AMOUNT *FOR* COMMUNITY

A healthy nation practices a holistic world-view. Higher amounts of goods and services are not beneficial to a nation in the presence of academic, intellectual, curricular, and research fragmentation. Those high amounts of goods and services are irrelevant when a nation reduces cosmology to astrophysics. Allowing students to learn and know as they please in a distributional requirement program does no good even when the nation has higher Gross Domestic Product. Cosmos is the core curriculum: specialization is always specialization only *for* the core curriculum, and the core curriculum is *of* specialization. Phenomenology reintroduces specialization into the core curriculum when jobs have been emptied from that curriculum, from liberal arts and sciences.

Phenomena are areas of work, and cosmology is general education as the context for work. The productive, healthy nation first of all educates people to understand the liberal arts and sciences as basic to their jobs. This provides us with the fundamental picture of persons as generalists, orienting whatever and however much they produces as workers. What does this involve on a day-to-day basis? Production amount must be *for* the people, including respect for home, client, and nature.

People must go to work, even if their job is in the same building and they go downstairs from where they live. This may be in the big city or a smaller town. The worker is a certain distance from and has to deal with the consumer. Individuals relate to the environment. Constructing buildings for the consumer, whether residences or commercial, can be almost painless or a gigantic financial and marketing nightmare. Implicit in each of these issues is the notion of the person as person and worker. Producing a high quantity of goods and services does not solve problems concerning the person, worker, consumer, or ecology. I shall consider the following points: (1) distance between home and work; (2) distance between worker and client; (3) knowing the client; (4) worker and nature; (5) preleasing and Co-Being.

1. Workplace Should Be Near Home

Rodney Ferguson and Eugene Carlson indicate that distance between work and home ought be reasonable.[1] Ideally, people should be able to live, work, and play within walking distance of each activity. On the practical side this may be difficult. However, it benefits society less and less in the long term if workers have to travel longer and longer distances to work. The individual who drives becomes tired and may often arrive late due to traffic jams, and productivity suffers. A nation producing larger amounts of goods and services loses in the long run if are people are having difficulty getting to work because of distances. The higher quantities may or may not be produced by individuals late for work. Yet, it does little good if many workers are arriving to work on time and having only nominal problems at the office or factory, with hundreds of thousands experiencing travel problems and contributing to productivity decline.

Phenomenologically, the distance between work and home can mean that the relation of two distinctly different places. If society assumes that two or more places must necessarily be distinct and therefore two or more fundamentally different spaces, then the worker has the responsibility to make a goal of traveling from one space that is inherently different from another space. The longer the distance to travel, the faster the trip has to be in order to leave reasonably early and not arrive late for work. The issue of transportation becomes a highly important factor. The worker thinks less and less of what to do to produce at work, or things to do at home, but more and more of the many obstacles to overcome when and if traffic becomes a problem. At the end of this section I point out the advantage of mass transportation.

The notion of Co-Being involves reintroducing discreet locations into and integrated residential areas. In this way, home and work become closer, and we can begin speaking, if not about walking to work, then of the distance as less and less a problem. I argue that the best scenario is usually for work to be generally within a residential area, certainly never more than ten or fifteen miles away. The farther the distance, the greater the difficulties of getting from point A to point B.

The issue of distance between work and home is having an effect on society. In a number of instances, state governments in the United States are encouraging, or even demanding car pools because of the Clean Air Act of 1990. This cuts down on the number of cars on the road, even if it does little to cut distance. Five or six people have a better chance of arriving to work on time, and in somewhat better condition than if each drove alone. Some companies offer vans or buses to ease the travel for every potential driver.

Traffic is not confined to workers traveling from home to work. Some states take any heavy traffic seriously and look upon the single passenger car or one-car-one-person notion as damaging to society. These states have instituted High Occupancy Vehicle (HOV) roads, which drivers may use only with other passengers in the same car.

Heavy traffic, whether general or work-related, has begun to take its toll on California. Think back a decade or so. California was the nation's suburb, with everyone wanting to leave their state to move to the Golden State. But just as suburbs become crowded after enough people opt for living outside the city, so California has begun to see the consequences of millions moving to it and traveling its highways. Instinctively, more and more people want to live in places where they do not encounter maddening traffic, especially to and from work. Thus, they have reversed the trend toward California.

Some may feel that the shift from autos to mass transit is helpful. I concur. An eastern state is attempting to build fewer roads and more rail lines, thus trying to persuade drivers to switch to trains. Los Angeles recently introduced a subway line, however short. This is something of a next step, if you will, in the transition from autos to mass transit.

We have known that air pollution from auto exhaust is bad and is getting worse. Attempting a remedy, newer fuels and better cars have been part of a long-term strategy to give us cleaner air. A recent innovation is the electric car. The electric car's main advantage is the total lack of exhaust (I ignore for this volume the possibility of greater amounts of hazardous by-products and waste we do see specifically as air pollution from exhausts). Theoretically and practically, millions of such cars on the road would mean less pollution in the air. However, the electric car is only part of the solution. The bigger problem is traffic and too much time in travel. Millions of clean cars still equals millions of cars causing traffic jams. With people getting out of their cars and into mass transit, the electric car becomes an antique, and the rail system the future.

Long trips to and from work inevitably affect home as well as work. This is no surprise, because family life cannot be divorced from work. With more and more time spent traveling between home and work, productivity is not the only thing that suffers. Spouses are forced to spend less and less time with each other at home, and, some may argue, more importantly, parents are compelled to spend equally little time with their children. With so much time required for driving long distances between work and home, workers leave home earlier than they wish and arrive in the evenings later than most want.

2. Cities Should Prevent Urban Sprawl

High productivity does little good if community disintegrates and the urban areas become meaningless sprawls. When we speak of workers having to travel long distances for work, this generally implies that they live far from work in an urban sprawl. If work and family are harmed by long travel, then everything associated with family likewise declines. This includes community. Herman E. Daly and John B. Cobb[2] are increasingly concerned with designing cities for people. These cities or communal areas would bring together all major human activities and institutions within a common border. Residents should know their neighbors. Ideally, most if not all should also share in community affairs.

It does not do anyone any good when a nation produces larger quantities of goods and services when so many workers are spending excessive time away from home and community. Individuals are more than workers or producers. Intersubjectivity reintroduces work into community and shows that work is more than just output: work is the enriching of the community and family. Emptying community and family of their productive aspects forces a society to look at community and family as virtually expendable and work as mere production of objects devoid of human meaning. I can apply Ricoeur here.

Ricoeur[3] points out that subject and object are fundamentally related in intersubjectivity. In the present context, we would say goods and services are fundamentally intersubjective, communal, social; no object, good, or service is apart from its social constraints. Each amount of output must be *for* Co-Being, and Co-Being is *of* the output. The community requires goods and services for survival and progress, but this output quantity must be within the context of social benefit: output quantity and kind must be *for* intersubjectivity. A society which emphasizes output, often does not even hint about the need to reintroduce object as quantity of output into subject (community and family). Such emphasis might assume that output is alone the important notion and ignore even a Cartesian, albeit inadequate, attempt to unite two separate substances. Person and work, general and specialized learning, mean general education is an economic area. What does it profit if society produces, but harms itself? Society is *of* productivity, but productivity is *fo*r people.

The computer age may be a harbinger of reducing the distance between home and work. Technological innovation making it possible for people to work at home has done something interesting. If ancient society meant the worker worked at or near home, and industrial society pulled home and work far apart, the computer may be doing something amazing: showing that home and work are not inherently distinct efforts. In the future, we may not all have or work with computers at home. However, the computer is showing that we can work at home, that employment and residence need not be in two distinctly different locations. With more former workers now working for themselves instead of their former companies, it is likely that, even without computers, people will see that home and work are not two contradictory or incompatible notions.

3. New England Banker

How close should the worker be to the client? From the perspective of Ron Suskind, the idea of the New England Banker[4] has meant that the bankers lend only to those individuals whom they can see from their windows. This notion carries a powerful statement about commerce. It says commerce is irreducible to commercialism or mere production. The producer is producing a good or service for a neighbor, a member of the community and not just a customer with money to burn. Important as is the idea of making money and producing for the client, many producers feel rightly that there is another side to work: work as enrichment of the community, work as the relationship between members of a family or extended family.

Many banks throughout New England produced lent and tried to collect for any customer with a seemingly good project. Most such banks failed because productivity for them was simply lending and recovering on loans. In short, banking was reducible to commercialism. One bank slowed down, considered its local responsibilities, its future, its capabilities, and the customer. As a result, its loans were made only with great care, and most did not default. Here, productivity was seen as a part of the community's well-being instead of the possibility of big money lent out for big returns. Big money looks good on paper, but it can mean future disaster.

The fast-lane banker appears to be helping the economy. The increasing GDP seems to do well with billions being lent, big projects going on, and lots of high rises, malls, and other properties being developed. On paper, the vast quantities of goods and services for an overheated economy give the impression, for the moment, of great prosperity. But looks can deceive, and the crash can be sudden. If economic trends suddenly turn and people cannot pay their way, all these high-powered investments turn sour and billions cannot be returned on loans. The small banker wins, the big bankers lose.

We know that many workers have to be far from their clients and indeed never personally see the consumer. Most big corporations produce for consumers around the world. In these cases, however, the astute corporation establishes decentralized, regional offices with local administrations and management culturally linked with local residents or consumers. Business is more than business, commerce more than commerce. Co-Being means business or commerce is community oriented. Workers are more than technicians. Like the bankers watching out for their workers and community, producers are not just technicians. Good producers are persons who produce within the context of healthy symbolism. They produce a quantity for their own good and that of their clients.

4. Each Client Is Cultural

The previous section gives a hint about the worker's cultural acknowledgment of the consumer. From the intersubjective perspective, clients are irreducible to a source of money; every client is a human being and part of a local culture, often distinct from the worker or at least the managers back home at headquarters.

Too often, the graduate school of business has been training the expert, the professional, while ignoring the producer's and, more importantly, the consumer's social and cultural nature. Being a technician is insufficient. Again, lived history becomes crucial. Many individuals throughout the world take religion, custom, languages, and tradition more seriously than a technician may think. Some graduate schools of business have begun to see that clients are more than spenders and buyers. Every individual has feelings, purpose, and self-respect. Each is a person. Business is more than the objective producing and selling of a product as an object to a client as the final object.

Everyone is involved. Producers are intersubjective, having their identity in terms of the other person. Producers and consumers are Co-Being instead of two distinct objects, one making money or profit through the other only as spender. Commerce must be a community activity, whatever the cultural or communal differences between worker and consumer. Thus, newer courses in business schools enable the student to be more than a technician. Sophisticated MBAs will approach the foreign client as a consumer with certain cultural requirements. Successful business professionals allow themselves to empathize with a foreign people and invite the foreign client to share what is good, desirable and perhaps necessary from the producer's perspective.

Most people in the Middle East know several Middle Eastern languages such as Arabic, Hebrew, Greek, Armenian. Most Europeans are familiar with French, German, English. It would be convenient for Americans if the world spoke more and more English. That often is the case, but, on other occasions, familiarity with language cannot hurt. No individual exists, produces, or buys in a cultural vacuum. Thus, business schools are beginning to incorporate courses in political, economic and cultural issues. What good does it do for the nation to produce higher quantities of goods that it cannot export because the producer does not understand foreign governments, ideals, fears, or histories? If other countries have certain business strategies and concepts, understanding these will mean a better business climate in the United States in the long term. We would be able to produce more, because our workers are then able to sell more abroad.

Understanding foreign cultures does not mean Americans must have two or more official languages. I am not arguing against English as our official language. We can learn English for our own cultural identity. Our business schools can then help their students learn foreign languages to the extent that such languages would help in doing business in other countries. Even if a businessperson must behave in certain ways in foreign countries in order to do better business, such as speak a different language, it does not follow that the American must do these things in our own country. We have our codes and mores, and other nations their own. Each nation's businesspeople may do as the Romans do when in Rome, but in their own country, they do their own thing. If Americans use a certain kind of money in a foreign country, this does not mean that we must make that money one of two or more officials currencies in America.

Liberal arts and sciences have been fighting an uphill battle in trying to tell us that being a technician is not enough: the worker is a human being. If continuing education experts have been emphasizing this for the adult worker, the idea of reintroducing the worker into the person is now receiving a warmer reception in business schools that teach professionals competing for foreign markets.

The sociology of work has been focusing on the fact that work is not the crass exchange of goods or services for money. Social, ethical, and moral constraints are the bounds within which technique is practiced. Sociologists of work have been indicating those truths independent of applied phenomenologists, who speak of intersubjectivity as basic to technique and commerce. The meaning is the same. National well-being is more than production amount, deeper than the worker as worker or technical expert. An expert may be able to do, to produce in a given job. But co-workers and clients are not solely co-technicians, and clients are not just recipients of production. The co-worker is a person and must be treated within certain social and ethical bounds. Clients do not just receive goods and services: etiquette, morals, and political considerations put restrictions on any economic exchange.

Thus, applied phenomenology makes the point that a job is more than doing something. Persons are the personal or interpersonal context for work. What persons are, how they live, behave, or otherwise conduct themselves are not indifferent or divorced from what they do at work. If a person lives in a way that is harmful, this could well affect work. Those who are obese, gamblers, loners, sexists, or racists could well become a problem for themselves and the client. The idea of liberal arts is that a worker must first learn to be as holistic a person as possible so that ethical and social constraints will orient work. No individual is a disembodied worker. No work is work alone: it is the work for personality, for intersubjectivity. Producing an amount means doing so for a social context, not just an objective biological organism.

5. Nature

Emphasis on higher GDP is harmful if it hurts nature. It does society no good to produce higher output when this production simply looks on nature as raw material for exploitation. Ricoeur would maintain that the object is nature as such, to be seen as for the community. The amount of goods and services must be *for* the human being and not a disembodied quantity. Community, individuality, and family are *of* nature in that people are partly natural. Every person exists in the environment. Conversely, the environment is *for* people in two ways: it is raw material to be transformed into beneficial quantities of goods and services;

but it is also beauty to be preserved for its own sake. As beauty, the environment means that the natural object is for the community, person, and family in the most general sense. The environment is part of our lived world and not to be changed in any form for utilitarian purposes. Nature is irreducible to raw material, commercialism, or the market. Thus, nature exists partly for the taking and partly as our material environment for enjoyment and beauty.

More poetically, intersubjectivity means nature is external for commerce and less external, more internal, for communal and psychological tranquility. This view suggests that nature is more complex than either environmentalists or traditional (anti-ecological) business people conceive of it. Nature is not just external. We are to subdue some of it for goods and services, and live with all remaining parts as more closely related to us. Both commercial and noncommercial aims must be reintroduced within community, with business as community-oriented, and nonbusiness purposes a more intimate aspect of the orientation.

This holistic view of commerce allows us to reintroduce domination of nature into a life where we blend with the environment. To dominate need not mean to destroy, or even to transform every piece of our resources into profit. A person might suggest that domination is Western thinking, and that the East tells us to live with instead of dominating nature. However, Western thinking and spirituality do not just mean dominion over nature. Let us not stereotype Western thought as monolithically anti-nature. Jewish and Christian traditions remind us that the universe belongs to God, that God rested on the Sabbath, and is our guide. We are told to look at how peaceful the birds are in the air, and lilies are in the field. They are not concerned with what will come, and we should be like them. Judaism and Christianity have mysticism. That qualifies the West to be somewhat like the East. People should use resources for reasonable, limited benefit, and not feel the need to constantly transform everything in the material world for commerce. We need not only produce or have greater amounts of production.

Among the items that many top business schools are teaching to their graduate students is a respect for the environment. MBA programs at Illinois Institute of Technology's Stuart School of Business, University of Illinois at Chicago, Northwestern University's Kellogg School of Management, The University of Texas at Dallas, and Boston University School of Management, include topics on environment. No longer can the business expert only take from nature, produce, sell, and not think about what happens when consumers discard old goods. Ecology is high on the list of things that commerce students learn. This reflects the general attitude in society toward a more informed ecological sensitivity. If the environment is not something from which to escape as in religious asceticism, nature is also not for the sake of making money. Within Judaism and Christianity, in particular, the world belongs to God. Therefore, the children of God must love, care for, and use the environment for spiritual reasons as a whole.

These spiritual directions enable commerce to occur as long as we do not carelessly take from nature.

The Cartesian view isolating subject from object is grounds for suggesting that nature is external and deserves little if any spiritual, intersubjective interpretation. Yet, phenomenology reminds us that there is no real externality; all nature is within a spiritual, human, possibly divine parameter. Implicit in this view is that in ravaging nature, one is really harming people, for nature gives us at least part of life. Co-Being sees nature as an object for intersubjectivity in two ways: we take from nature and produce goods and services only in amounts for people; and we otherwise wonder about, love, and appreciate natural beauty without having to transform it into goods and services. Thus, nature is for both work and personalism, both production and nonproduction.

6. Preleasing and Our Social Nature

When applied phenomenology seeks to reintroduce environment into social (and religious) values, this concerns what developers do in building high-rises for office and residential occupancy. The broader issue involves the philosophy of constructing shelter: its producer, buyer, financial situations, and dangers.

Throughout history, civilization has built shelter primarily when human beings needed a place to live, work, and play. Usually, society did not first produce dwelling places and empty objects in true Cartesian fashion, and then seek to find consumers to whom to sell them. In most cases, intersubjectivity has meant that the individuals who would use the building were either the ones constructing it or closely associated with the construction process. But the commodification of space above land resulted in our high-rise problem.

At the outset, I should emphasize that I am not justifying high-rise construction even if it is financially secure. Financial security cannot be the major criteria for building a high-rise. High-rises usually do not contribute to a sense of community. My point is that the high-rise glut represents a worst-case scenario involving production amount for the sake of increasing GDP instead of amount (object) *for* the person (subject). When quantity of production becomes an end in itself, such excarnation creates social and ecological problems. These problems occur at a time when no financial concerns exist. Construction builds high-rises, buyers buy and use them. Social and ecological difficulties occur and force us to juxtapose some human elements to the potential hazards. But excarnate construction can compound the difficulties by adding monetary loss.

That issue involves several points. The Cartesian perspective considers construction and development companies looking at land and space as divisible. The companies break ground, fill in the foundation, and put up the high rise. They are filling in what they perceive as empty space beneath and above ground.

For Cartesian dualism, space above ground is something humanity fills, and not a part of the ecosystem within which we live. This view starts by distinguishing construction company, market or consumer, and environment. The construction company completes the project and then looks for the customer to fill the empty spaces or apartments. This view considers nature as raw material. Producers or construction companies only produce product quantity for selling, and the consumer only buys; wholeness, community or intersubjectivity does not exist. Existence is reduced to a business transaction. But this transaction, in turn, begins by ignoring instead of considering and including the market or buyer.

This makes marketing paramount. Financial disaster can and does follow if few or no customers come in. The aim is to put up the high-rise, whether for apartments or offices, and hope that the society can, in Newtonian fashion, fill up the voids. All existence and relations are strictly juxtapositions of people to spaces. The construction and real estate corporations find themselves in positions of researching the market by analyzing demographic and other matters relating to who is where and needs space.

The producer is only producer to get profit, and the consumer is only the physical resident or employee and source of money. A building is therefore simply a commodity that we construct in order to make money. Little if anything indicates that people are linked to each other, the past, present, or future. Lived history, an idea of lived location and place, does not exist. For the most part, people buying apartments will be doing so to live in one place. The producer is not overly concerned with the community of which the consumer is part. If the high-rise is an office complex, the producer is not thinking about the employees' residence. Few high-rise projects are built as packages, so to speak, where work, play, residence, and so forth are integrated. Applied phenomenology sees things differently.

Intersubjectivity starts with people as communal and not commodities, producers, consumers, or apart from nature. Phenomenologically, most building ought to be done by the structure's future residents or workers, or by those closely associated with these individuals. Co-Being begins with the community and manifests its needs, instead of by building a high-rise and then marketing it. At the very least, high-rise builders who build only after having leased the space are doing better philosophy and business than those who start only with the space and then advertise. From the phenomenological perspective, any construction project is the community's project as such. Construction should be Co-Being at least in terms of preleasing. To paraphrase Abraham Lincoln, a building is of, by, and for the community that is seeking a place. Thus, intersubjectivity sees the space below, on, and above land as the community's and never as mere geometry. Amount for buyer, would mean not only an appropriate quantity instead of higher GDP, but a number that originates with the producer and consumer meeting and the customer indicating appropriate shelter needs.

A phenomenological approach starts with the social order and thereby averts future financial disaster. When we look at the modern high-rise going up, we probably see one of two major things. The onlooker can observe an office or residence going up and the developer seeking clients: the building is "now leasing" In other words, the producer has begun by constructing something and has no future financial commitment from buyers. But the safer project involves a company putting up a building for its use. In that case, the onlooker usually sees a sign (or article in the paper) indicating that a corporation is constructing a headquarters or other kind of building. The producer's finances are relatively safe through commitment, and the banker making the huge loan is relatively secure if the corporation is able to repay the loan. The high-rise initially belongs to and manifests a corporate move; it means IBM, CBS, GM, Xerox, or Podunk International has started the project. This high-rise is being built for a company, a market, that has begun the construction project, and the developer will not need to market the completed building. Co-Being triumphs here. Preleased construction means buyer and builder are there together, so that the finished project is utilized and no person gets financially hurt. Without Co-Being, the developer or construction company has the burden of first building, then finding lessors. With minimal Co-Being—preleasing—financial risk is low. Limits on quantification should not be alien to capitalism.

Phenomenological capitalism means we must reintroduce excarnate or extra-social quantification into the cultural context. Reintroduction of quantification into the social context rejects two extremes of capitalist production. One distortion involves reducing national well-being to mere quantity of goods and services. This distortion identifies the nation's health with increasing GDP. But higher GDP is meaningless when we have unemployment, underemployment, and employee dissatisfaction. We must reintroduce GDP into community. GDP is only *for* people; people are only *of* a GDP.

The other extreme means insufficient quantification. This distortion would have us produce so few goods and services that our quality of life becomes all but primitive. A quality of life requires sufficient quantities of goods and services. Phenomenologically, the capitalist system requires the quantity-community continuum.

True, construction remains quantity. Maybe society does not need another high-rise, shopping mall, or more construction. Social and ecological problems might well ensue. But at the very least, some minimal, token intersubjectivity producer and consumer being there together from the start can result in extremely low financial risk for the bank and producer. The corporation may well be commodifying air space and doing the other kinds of damage mentioned, but at least it may avoid becoming part of the high-rise glut where office and residential spaces stand half empty, and losses mount to hundreds of millions. In construction, amount ought be only *for* the person as producer and buyer instead of only proliferating buildings. When it is *for* the person, the consumer has initiated the process, and become committed to its future. The producer is not just building adequate numbers for the sake of preventing excess: sufficient numbers must begin with the consumer's commitment to the building's future.

Even if building is at the smaller level, say, the family home, the financial situation becomes safer when the construction is sold at the time of starting. Thus, phenomenology argues that we reintroduce construction into community, or at least single home for single buyer, in order to maintain intersubjectivity and prevent financial crisis. Interestingly, taking our social nature into account helps resolve fiscal difficulties. To begin construction before leasing leads to potential money problems if the buyers never appear; to begin building simultaneously with leasing and signing the buyer prevents headaches. It relates the consumer with the producer or product in an immediate sense. In phenomenological fashion, this shows that producer, product and consumer are one. Applied phenomenology allows us to see that marketing ought to be reintroduced into social relations or lived history in order to gain maximum benefit.

Intersubjectivity in high-rise or any construction perceives the project as ours, including producer and consumer, and not just the producer's or mine. In lived history, construction manifests a people seeking to better themselves, and not just a developer seeking money by going through complex and difficult marketing. Again, it is interesting that when we first build a high-rise or other building and then serially looks for customers and hopes for financial profit instead of loss, the developer is practicing only serial or chronological succession of events or *Historie*. This is disorientation, or dis-orientation. However, lived history's simultaneousness of producer, buyers and product means *Geschichte*, or lived history. For lived history, we reintroduce the serial into nonserial enrichment. But there is another problem with preleasing or a company building for itself.

Let us assume a construction company preleases a project. It builds something for a consumer with whom it has signed an agreement. The construction company need not first build and then look for a customer. Any building we see going up is indeed the company's own edifice, and everyone will be happy when it is completed. With financial risk at its lowest, the construction company loses nothing. The nation is served well, as a building has successfully gone up and workers are now productive within its walls. Yet, some might take quantity more seriously than this.

By definition, the country does better economically if, for example, the same company contracts with a construction company to build another place to which present workers will move. In other words, the corporation is unhappy for some reason, such as local taxes, crime, and so forth, and seeks to leave its present location. Assuming most of its work force agrees to move, the nation's economic well-being appears to be improving with yet another preleased building going up, especially if someone purchases the land or building that will soon be vacated. We think it is good news, with more jobs for construction, and more jobs for all those other workers for whom the company that is moving is now the customer.

Yet, the story is different. If companies build and pick up and move time and again, the quantity of production increases, but national values suffer. One point that many people seem to desire is continuity, tradition, and stability of physical location. Excitement of a newly opened store soon vanishes, and how many vacant stores are there in empty malls where commercialism was the only factor? However, a building that has identified itself with a physical, geographical location, and the company committed to the values and meaning of a parcel of land can soon become a tourist attraction.

If, as I suggest, Co-Being becomes preleasing, Co-Being can also be the perpetuation of tradition. The company seeks to say that its building manifests a work force instead of empty walls to be marketed for customers, but its work force itself manifests more than production. The workers and company manifest a solid tradition or history, a name of an institution. Current workers are keeping alive the company name, at a given physical location, and thereby the workers are more than workers, but are part of a long tradition of humanity.

Ultimately, phenomenological cosmology reintroduces production amount into community, family, clients, and nature. Excarnating production amount from those cultural contexts results in serious human problems even when production is high.

The healthy nation attempts to have workers work near home, spend time with their families, respect their clients, build projects with preleasing, and acknowledge tradition and nature. Producing large amounts of goods and services does not benefit a nation when workers spend excess time traveling to work, ignore family and community, see the client only as consumer, envision construction only for the sake of money and ignore preleasing and tradition, and see nature only as raw material. Production amount is only *for* community and nature; community and nature are *of* production amount.

THREE

PRODUCT DESIGN *FOR* USER

In Chapter Two I argued that the phenomenological approach to production amount means producing an amount of products or objects *for* humanity, instead of just higher quantities as discreet entities distinct from people. This chapter tells us that even if society produces only a sufficient quantity of goods and services, the reasonable quantity can be harmful if each good and service is designed without the user in mind. User-friendly design is necessary for each good and service if the operator or user is to use each one with safety, pleasure, and productivity. Design itself must be *for* the subject and never a distinct concept from the user. The term "user- or human-friendly" is directly phenomenological, for it means a design *for* the person, a design directly related to the individual's limits and needs.

If, as phenomenologists argue, object and subject are not two distinct entities juxtaposed to each other, then a phenomenological approach to design goes deeper into this relationship and says we must reintroduce design into the user. Design and the user are not discreet concepts but are fundamentally unified. Where Cartesian dualism speaks of the subject-object problem, user-friendly design criticizes the design-user problem or dualism when design ignores the user. For Ricoeur, users would be basic to the design; we do not design something, and then add it to something called the user.

The Cartesian perspective empties design from the user so that design and user are two distinct entities. However, phenomenology reintroduces design into the operator, showing that design is incarnate instead of excarnate.

1. User-Friendly: Intersubjective Design

Take a look at any human-made object in history. The ancient spear, writings or drawings inside caves, whatever clothing people have worn, or any vehicle for transportation have all been designed for the maximum convenience, comfort, and safety of the operator. Human nature probably has an instinct for producing a good or service that does not harm the user. People have built dwelling places, printing equipment, utensils for eating, or any artifact in war or peace that can be used with relative ease and security for the user. If the item is for war and is meant to kill the enemy, the soldier using it must be able to use it with safety for himself or herself. Only the enemy is to get hurt or killed. Even here, we are not to only technically kill or hurt the enemy. Nuclear bombs are at least debated, and chemical weapons or biological warfare banned: killing the enemy must be ethical in the process. Humanity will likely debate the ethics and morals of bombing Hiroshima until time ends.

Language is developed in the same way. Anthropologists, archaeologists, and others researching the past will have great difficulty decoding ancient civilizations' symbols and meanings. But the researchers' comfort was obviously not the original designer's purpose. Languages and other symbols were done for the sake of the people using them to do so with relative ease. Again, codes during war are a different story. Teachers teach the soldier about a code and how to fool the enemy. Otherwise, a language is made so that it is as easy as possible for the native population to learn to communicate.

Closely related to language are songs, poetry, and all forms of written and oral literature. People who write songs, poetry, or any form of entertainment take into account the fact that the audience knows certain things about the culture and about human nature, and therefore can comprehend certain things and not others. Communication is almost never intended to confuse the listener.

Throughout history, designers have assumed that the best way of designing something is to consider the audience, user, or people who will hear, see, feel, or otherwise do something with the good and service. All of this has been done mostly by instinct. Human beings find themselves in a culture and possess a sense of what members of the culture can and cannot do. People are fundamentally Co-Being, aiming at the ease and relative security of other people with whom they are not at war.

Does this mean people are inherently good rather than evil? On the whole, it would appear that most individuals care about others. Some may be criminally or anti-socially inclined, but these may well be in the minority, or else civilization might well cease quite soon. Most individuals seem eager or willing to get along.

In modern times, goods and services have become more complicated. The formal field of user-friendly design comes to us from the emerging science or discipline of Human Factors or ergonomics. How do engineers design a safe airline cockpit, automobile, bus, train, television, nuclear reactor or computer and software? Designers may not hate people, but commercialism, ignorance, and other forms of neglecting the audience have often resulted in harm to the user through unsafe design. User-friendly design attempts to correct that situation by doing research into people's biological, psychological, social, and other dimensions; limits; and capabilities.

No longer are we developing simple languages and other goods and services that individuals may use with minimal training. Computer languages, the nuances and problems of human development, speed, electronics, and advances in science and technology seem to have conspired in forcing us to begin intensive and extensive research into human nature to determine the best design for goods and services. To produce in today's and tomorrow's increasingly complex world, the design of goods and services yet unimagined must be friendly or *for* the subject, and not just a technical possibility.

Thus, humanity has evolved from an instinctive to a more deliberate or conscious effort toward product design. Taking the audience into account is necessary to developing and selling a complex product in a complex economy and society. The instinct of being good to our neighbors hopefully continues to exist. This instinct is all the more important in attempting to sell something to them as clients. Salespersons know that their survival could well depend on selling not just to friend, but also to foe. Hence, knowing people is as important as ever, and perhaps more important.

2. Social Relations

User-friendly design shows Husserl's idea that the individual I meet is someone like me[1] instead of only a biological or even inanimate object. But what does it mean to assume that the individual I meet is an object or a something?

The phenomenologist argues that social relations is the basic context for every human being. Each of us meets others every day. How do we know others are persons like ourselves? In any social activity, I am only encountering others, and, for the moment, relating only to others instead of dealing with an object I have designed for them.

I can consider others as only skin, bones, or biology. I can look at others and feel that the only way to define them as a persons is to consider them only from the theoretical, biological perspective. Because others have arms, legs, and all the portions of a human body, I am classifying them within biological characteristics and only then concluding that they are human beings like me. In all this procedure, I have reduced others to anatomic components and concluded that they are like me because they look and behave as I do. They and I are human beings because of our similar anatomic properties. I may not even think of comparing them with myself. Their anatomic similarities to me help me understand that they are human beings. They conform to the scientific, reductive, anatomic idea of human nature. They are human beings because their physical nature conforms to an abstraction.

I would be implying that this method takes time to consider each individual I meet as a human being. In each instance of a new encounter, I first reduce others to anatomy, compare them with biological characteristics, and then conclude they are human beings. Such a perspective consists of a mediate or mediated approach to considering the other as a person. I see the individual, then apply rigorous intellectual method in determining whether that individual compares with, say, a biology text system of anatomic characteristics in order for me to believe the other is a human being.

Suppose the individual I meet has only one arm, or only part of a leg, or is otherwise physically different from what biology claims is the physically normal anatomy. Imagine the person is of a different color or sex. What then is the human being? It is not wrong to say that an abstract, theoretical standard of anatomic characteristics indicative of a human being exists. Any biology text implies that people should have two arms, two legs, and other anatomic characteristics. Anything else would mean the individual is physically handicapped. Assume also that behavioral standards exist, deviation from which means the person we meet is mentally or emotionally handicapped.

However, taking the mediated approach to determining who is a human being in social relations can result in a serious problem. We would need several theoretical standards ranging from normal or abnormal. Given the possibility of an infinite number of ways people can differ physically and mentally, an infinite number of theoretical standards would need to exist. That, obviously, borders on the ludicrous. It suggests that in meeting anyone, I would have to spend the better part of my life simply mediating what I see with a theoretical standard an infinite number of standards.

Phenomenology solves this problem. From the intersubjective perspective, social relations is much simpler in determining the humanity of the individual I meet. The phenomenologist argues that a person I meet is already, without reflection, abstraction, theory or rigorous intellectual research, a human being just as am I. This approach entails immediacy over mediacy as the means of determining in social relations the person's humanity. As I encounter others, I immediately sense they are human beings as am Each individual is fully and completely someone like me, no different, no distinction.

Additionally, empathy plays an important role in this immediacy. Encountering others is not just a cognitive or sensory experience. I empathize with the others as persons. I feel and sympathize that the others are persons like me. Immediacy means that I immediately, without thinking or comparing them with a biological model, feel with them that they are human beings like me. I am emotionally aware of those human beings.

Whereas mediacy starts determining other's humanity by comparing their physical characteristics with biological standards, immediacy begins such determination in terms of sensing that others are persons as am I. My initial consideration is not their physical normality or abnormality, not whether they have both arms and legs, but pre-reflectively, pre-theoretically that they are human beings as am I. Any difference in their anatomy is secondary. Once I see others, I immediately know, acknowledge, and accept their humanity, without having to spend any time in rigorous examination of their physical or mental state.

This phenomenological approach has implications for racial, sexual, and religious assumptions. Others I encounter are first of all like me; they are not first of all a different color, creed, or gender. Phenomenoligists do not ask anything when they encounter others. They do not seek to know if others are male or female, Jew or Gentile, black, or white. Those characteristics do not constitute the immediate humanity of others. Additionally, the notion of Co-Being does not stop to consider others' mental states. Others are first human beings like me, and not mentally impaired. Should others have differences in color, gender, or religion, these would enter later and be irrelevant as to any determination of their nature as human beings. And should others be mentally impaired, this, too, enters later and is equally immaterial as to any conclusion about their nature as a human being.

Moreover, phenomenology enables us to feel and show respect toward animals, plants, and, indeed, the inanimate world. If I feel or emphathize with other people that they are like me, I feel that I should have respect for all existence. I am emotionally involved in acknowledging the value of animals, which, among all nonhumans, are probably most like people. We should not compare animals with a biological model to see if the moving thing I encounter is an animal. Plants are less like us in the biological kingdom. Yet, because plants are part of existence, I must feel respect toward them and not have to compare them to a model. The inanimate world remains. I need not compare rocks, water, any land, or the air, with a biological, chemical, or physical model in order to determine that these are to be valued. All existence is of value. Nothing in the environment lacks value and the demand that I respect and live with it. If something is not a person like me, it does not matter. That form of life or existence a different form of existence, but existence and environment nonetheless. I may be able to feel with an animal. If I cannot empathize with a plant, with air, water, and land, I certainly can and must feel for it and live with it.

In social relations, phenomenologists tell us that in meeting others, we should take the immediate approach in determining if others are persons as we are. Their humanity is immediately real, never in need of rigorous theoretical examination or analysis. This humanity transcends any racial, religious, sexual, or impairment issue. Others are human beings as am I because they are human beings; their humanity is irreducible to biological and other characteristics, irreducible to theoretical and rigorous intellectual analysis. But what of developing objects and ideas for people?

3. Objects *for* Co-Being

If, as I argue, the phenomenological approach to social relations entails an irreducible approach to determining whether others are human beings as I am, I also have to take into account another inevitable event in life: individuals build or develop things for themselves and other human beings. No individual can exist in a world without nature, in a world without artifacts and language. What about the design of those artifacts and symbols?

Co-Being means we can consider basically two ways of designing something for people. One is only technical. Many modern items—road signs, computers and software, airline cockpits, nuclear reactors, modern military weapons, autos—and so on are some of history's simplest and most complex entities. The road sign is among the easiest technical items; the nuclear reactor control panel and military weapons are among the most complex, to say nothing of being the most dangerous. The simplest and the most complex require varying degrees of highest mathematical, and other scientific, and technical competence.

Let us say technicians design something for people whom they assume are not human beings. This involves the previous section's first notion: that the individual we meet is reducible to anatomy. Even a social relationship based on rigorous biological analysis suggests we take a good look at biology or anatomy. Faulty as that is, at least a person is thereby a biological entity similar to us. But the emphasis on design that ignores the user tends to look at biology as something less than belonging to a human being.

Reducing individuals to biology is not the way to proceed in determining their humanity in social relations; the same reductionism in product design results in serious consequences. To say that an object or idea is only to be perceived, sensed, heard, moved, touched, or memorized by a biological organism we would call an operator is faulty. A purely technical approach reduces the individual to arms, legs, eyes, ears, and other biological traits without taking their limits and capabilities into account. Thus, technicians see thenselves only as a mathematician, technician, scientist, or other type of doer unrelated to human beings. They put together nuts and bolts regardless of the person's ability to deal with them.

This presents a problem. Buttons are to be pushed; numbers, dials, lights, and other visual displays are to be seen; levers are only to be moved; noises and sounds only for hearing; temperature for feeling heat and cold; and spaces among objects only for physical or leg and arm movement. These instances are accidents waiting to happen because the designers ignore our human limits. The designers believe users are only skin, bones, brains, and movement, lacking human qualities and biological limits. For the perspective of Co-Being, technicians have done nothing to understand users' biological, social, or psychological characteristics.

While people are first of all people in social relations, they are indeed biological realities when dealing with objects and ideas. To operate an instrument, every individual is relatively reducible to sensorimotor characteristics. Technicians must take those characteristics into account and not build something that will move and generate sound, visual displays, and temperature. Technicians designing a machine as only a technical problem consider themselves as unrelated to other people; never a Co-Being. Perhaps they never consider even themselves as a being, butonly a technical expert. How many intellectuals in both art and science cannot communicate with people? I think too many are capable of this detachment.

As a result, technicians design cockpits in ways whereby pilots easily have accidents and planes go down. Those who design nuclear plants as the one at Three Mile Island consider the operator as just arms, legs, eyes, and ears. The product is then designed without considering human ability and limits, and accidents result. If the computer is built in a way that makes typing difficult, the design leads to more and more errors that are not the typist's fault. Software can present problems if the typist is unfamiliar with efficient language and, for a time, requires natural language. In each of these and similar cases where the machine is only a technical problem, the technicians reduce operators to the sum total of sensorimotor-memory processes and ignore detailed information about human bodily functions. Usera are degraded to something that only moves arms, sees, hears, moves legs, takes up space, and continues through time.

Descartes would say here that the design and user are two distinct realities, which we then have to juxtapose to each other. From a Ricoeurian perspective, we overcome this design-user dualism by reintroducing design into the user after technicians emptied the user of the design. For Schutz,[2] this would mean the engineer and user are a community, and the object's design ought be social rather than reducible. Phenomenologists do not see what Cartesians see, a design different from the user. Whereas the technicians' Cartesianism starts with the design as a technical juxtaposition of nuts and bolts and then adds this to users; phenomenologists start with the user-design unity. Design is a sociology or of design; it is a design only *for* the user. To see the design as a solely technical problem is to consider nuts and bolts, the control panel, and all visual displays and controls as thoroughly discreet objects separate from each other, and from the user.

The exclusively technological design means that the machine only does something, only performs, and therefore requires users to only move parts of their anatomy whether it hurts or kills. Things only do, people only do. In this sense, existence is reduced to the overcoming of time and space without any human qualities. Society only produces. But as phenomenology argues, what good does it do for a society to only produce when the operators become sick or injured, perhaps killed, when operating poorly designed machines? The healthy society and holistic cosmology involves producing with humanly designed machines. An unhealthy society considers the individual as only having to pull, push, look, see, hear, touch, feel simply produce, simply be trained to be mechanically capable.

Just as sensory deprivation chambers have shown us that subject is related to object, accidents in modern history with poorly designed machines have made manifest the fact that design itself is also related to user. Design cannot be indifferent to the operator. User-unfriendly design kills or at least injures. Modern history, with many airline crashes, nuclear disasters, and other accidents is the story of user-friendly design deprivation, proving that we cannot have discreet design juxtaposed to an equally discreet operator. History or social circumstances involving accidents are the broad, cultural version of the sensory deprivation experiment. Those circumstances are a subset of sensory deprivation.

The second way of designing a product is to make the design a social phenomenon. Fremont E. Kast, Richard A. Johnson, and James E. Rosenzweig[3] tell us a design is social. Social, cultural, and political dimensions are a major factor in the design. Phenomenologically, we reintroduce design or technology into the operator as intersubjectivity. Seeing the design means seeing the user's limits and capabilities. Whereas designing something as only a technical problem assumes the operator is reducible to skin and bones, user-friendly design assumes the operator is a human being like us. Hence, while social relations depends on an immediate acknowledgment of the other individual's humanity and does not require rigorous intellectual examination, design does.

In designing something, the user-friendly concept assumes that technicians design for a human being's limits and capabilities. If this is the case, the human being ought to be reduced to sensory motor-memory data and classification. This classification and reduction allows technicians to determine just how to design a machine or idea in order for the operator to be able to operate it for maximum productivity through maximum safety and comfort. If we assume that the user is a person, a human being like ourselves, it is necessary, in designing an object, to understand fully the individual's biological, social, and psychological dimensions. These are the things with which users will deal with the machine. In caring for users, in assuming they are persons like ourselves, we develop an object by scrutinizing their sensorimotor-memory capabilities and limits. Mediacy is no longer inappropriate, and spending time to see just what makes people tick is important time well-spent. Technicians who design user-friendly machines wish to help persons safely produce or otherwise relate to the human environment. The engineer believes operators are human beings with dignity and value. This belief translates into rigorous biological study of the operator, because the goal is no longer only social relations, but also design of an object to be used by the operator.

The more the Human Factors engineers analyze the human being, the more precise their measurements, the more they show their concern for the operator's value as a human being. Reduction as a means of determining a persons' humanity is unnecessary and time-consuming, leading to a dehumanizing and quantified person. Reduction as a means of determining the sensorimotor-memory limits and capabilities of the person we already pre-reductively assume to be a human being is a necessary sign of Co-Being for whom we are building a product. The Human Factors engineers thereby know how to design a product for the human being's safety and comfort. Spending even a short time analyzing biological characteristics to see if a person is a human being becomes a reductive, Cartesian error. I classify others as a biological entity like myself and therefore they are human beings. However, spending a great deal of time, money, and effort for classification, data, and scientific understanding of persons in order to design objects *for* them assumes the healthy, phenomenological concern for the operators, so that they will use a machine with minimal problems.

One example is the installation of computer software.[4] Suppose a corporation with many secretaries introduces its workers to a new software package. The computer experts install the new program and then find that the secretaries are having great difficulty with the software. What do the experts do? If the technicians assume that the software is irreversible and the secretaries are not human beings, then the company and installers force the secretaries to produce, to do, to be technicians themselves, and to learn the new software regardless of the difficulties they encounter. However, the computer experts can assume that all people are human beings, and that the secretaries are to be treated with respect.

As a result, the installers rethink the software language to make it more natural though less efficient for the time being. This allows the secretaries to acquire a feel for the program's logic and procedures. Computer experts bring in the new, less efficient program and, at the same time, interview the secretaries to learn something about their backgrounds. All this takes time, and that expenditure is necessary, because computer technicians know they are dealing with human beings and not just experts. If it turns out that many secretaries can handle a natural language better, then they are trained for that less efficient program, while others who can deal with it are allowed to work with the efficient program. It may be that some secretaries have had previous computer experience and can therefore handle efficient language.

This information would not be possible if the computer company assumed the worst. If the computer experts believed that people must be computer experts regardless of their needs, backgrounds, and experiences, the experts would obviously tell the secretaries that torture, suffering, and pain are the only way to go. This anti-intersubjective attitude results in less productivity, lower morale, and less loyalty to the company. Only when the computer experts see themselves as humans prior to being professionals, and similarly see the secretaries as persons prior to being technically competent secretaries, do the computer people relate at all to the secretaries' problems.

In assuming the individual is a human being as well as a technician, Human Factors experts do research in many human fields to determine how best to adapt the design for the user's bodily and emotive limits. But user-friendly design goes beyond even that. When technicians believe the operator is first of all a human being, they find, after scrutiny, that some people are biologically different in terms of their ethnicity. For example, Japanese are shorter than Americans. This insight is acknowledged because a Human Factors phenomenological approach respects the human being and considers any aspect of the operator that will affect the machine's operation. In this case, the problem is automobile design. With Japanese drivers being physically shorter, than their American counterpart, Human Factors technicians collect sufficient evidence about people from Japan to determine how best to design an auto that those individuals will drive.

Human Factors professionals assuming the individual is a human being needing respect. That respect translates into realizing that not all cars produced for sale will be the same. Those built for the United States and many other countries will have greater space between driver and pedals; those designed for Japan would have shorter spaces between driver and pedals.

In social relations, I do not need to do research to determine that others I meet are human beings like me. In developing objects and ideas for the individual I assume is a human being, I must expend much effort in measuring the arms, legs, movements, sight, hearing, and other physical and mental characterists so that the person will feel comfortable, safe, and satisfied in using an object or learning a software program. For Co-Being, Human Factors engineers design a machine *for* the user: the button is a button for a person with an ability to reach certain lengths with his arm; the visual display is a visual item for the human being to see in terms of certain visual capabilities and constraints. Distances from one place to another are spaces irreducible to mere distance or discreet space; they are, instead, spaces for the human being to move in terms of specific motor abilities and restrictions. The reason a dial is built instead of, a verticle series of numbers is because human beings see best when seeing a dial. Phenomenologists and Human Factors engineers concur that the design is meant to reflect the human being's nature and characteristics.

Thus, for Co-Being and Human Factors, the person is more than the sum of motions, sights, sounds, spaces, or climates. Each characteristic must be so calculated as to conform to a human being's physical and social contexts. Nothing is only out-there; nothing only occurs; nothing is only for the sake of producing or doing. Every design is such that the human being feels comfortable and happy relating to it. Sensations, motions, or data do not exist out of human context. No visual, auditory, or other object is excarnate or disembodied; for Ricoeur, every aspect of the machine or human environment is within the humanly embodied biological context. Barry F. Kantowitz and Robert D. Sorkin show that this constraint allows operators to optimize their relation to the machine.[5] David Stewart and Algis Mickunas point out that the better a design conforms to specific anatomic, sensorimotor limits, the more efficiently an operator we assume to be someone like us will perform and produce.[6]

Today, we put much emphasis on competence or performance over lifestyle. We ask whether the designers or any workers do a good job. But part of that good work is more than being at work to produce a technically acceptable product or service. A job is also dependent on designing a good or service that presents the fewest problems for the users. Workers are persons, not just technicians. If they smoke or drink or engages in any activity that would adversely affect them or others, this could impact either their work or life itself, The good or service is not only a technical problem whereby the designed product will function. Any item is relating to the operator and therefore requires the social context for orientation.

This difference between the only technical and the user-friendly is like the difference between Newtonian and Einsteinian physics. The difference can also be like Newtonian, Einsteinian, and Heisenbergian physics. Just as Newton saw people as passive observers of discreet bodies in space, the exclusively technical design sees individuals as only operators having to be trained for passive productivity at unsafe machines. Just as Einstein said objects, space, and time are relative to the observer, so phenomenologists and Human Factors engineers insist that design is relative to the user's limits and abilities. Like Werner Heisenberg, the phenomenologist and Human Factors engineers argue that the user has a definite impact upon the design; seeing the design means seeing the operator, who directly influences the design.

The typical Human Factors text looks like a biology or psychology text. Parts or chapters deal with sensorimotor capabilities. We find what the eyes, ears, nose, nerves, arms, legs, and body in general can and cannot do under varying circumstances. A chapter or two concern memory and understanding; most people learn natural language better than the more efficient numeric languages of sophisticated software. Inexperienced computer operators need to start with natural language; experienced operators can then graduate to more efficient abbreviations and commands. Thus, Human Factors tries not to impose efficient language on rookies.

With the typical Human Factors text involving biological, psychological, mathematical, physical, and social aspects of knowledge, Co-Being triumphs in the kind of people who are Human Factors specialists. They are familiar with biology, psychology, architecture, engineering, and related disciplines that go into designing any human artifact. Additionally specialists from each of these fields work together. Specialists are intersubjective, Co-Being, instead of only intellectual experts. They are human beings and Co-Being prior to their professional skills.

While this may sound trivial, its perspective is profound. In most instances today, specialists are a proud group and rarely consider working or cooperating with other kinds of specialists. Each group of professionals considers itself a group of experts in a field first, a group of technicians, before a collection of human beings. Co-Being has yet to triumph in those cases, but it has made a major triumph in Human Factors. The phenomenologist sees intersubjectivity in Human Factors because biologists will talk and share information with psychologists, engineers, architects, sociologists, and humanists unlike most departmentalized activity in the typical university campus. The phenomenologist notices that within the professional's Human Factors field, the design is ours and not just that of a particular specialist, especially a mathematician or engineer. The design belongs, in a technical sense, to the interdisciplinary, intersubjective group rather than to a group of specialists. Intersubjective professionalism means the experts or technicians with competence in a given field realize that they are part of the real world of other competences.

For Jack A. Adams, this holistic approach is toward making the design sufficiently safe to minimize error.[7] While every human environment is subject to Human Factors study, and while the user uses equipment at home, work, play, and all other places, the main place of concern seems, rightly, at work. Work is where society produces goods and services, and the more errors and accidents there, the less productivity for society. What good does it do for a society if there is increasingly high production with more and more accidents and deaths? The healthy society develops designs for the workplace so that the operator has the fewest possible accidents, errors, and other problems.

How does Human Factors study people? Human Factors researchers perform rigorous intellectual analysis of sensorimotor-memory capabilities, because they design objects and ideas for individuals assumed to be human beings. The present chapter, even this entire book, is not the place for extensive exposition about Human Factors research methods. Many Human Factors texts can supply that information. I will only indicate two items concerning that research and the assumptions underlying that work.

One research method deals with laboratory work. The Human Factors professionals want to know some things about human behavior and wish to have variables as true as possible. Individuals are brought in from the workplace, the real world, and are put through a number of tests to measure their biological and related dimensions. These can include the length of arms and legs, attention spans, how individuals move while seated under various conditions, the affect of noise and confusion on work, and so forth. These can also include the impact of lighting, color, climate, speed, and the ability to discipline oneself in the handling of dangerous equipment such as printing presses, cutting equipment, and other items that cannot be made less hazardous. The laboratory helps researchers determine how individuals react or interface with machinery under various circumstances.

Once this data is in, the researchers feel that the workplace will need to be designed in certain ways due to the worker's limits and abilities found in a sterile, non-work, controlled laboratory situation. The belief that the worker is a human being therefore has led the research to isolate the person from the workplace and to try to understand what individuals can and cannot do in physical situations outside work. But because work is a messy location and cannot be so sterile or isolated from life, the researchers, concerned about their fellow persons, do at least one other thing.

This second method is for the researcher to actually visit the workplace to see what people do during production. The Human Factors researcher is assuming that the worker is a human being involved in at least two situations. The controlled laboratory condition yields precise numbers, but the workplace is where the actual production and service occurs. By believing the users are human beings requiring more than one method of analysis in designing a product for them, the Human Factors professional is willing to go to the workplace and see what problems it has. We must know how people can move, see, hear, touch, and have accidents in a controlled situation, but it is also necessary to determine how to design things in a messy world where human beings with all their frailties and faults work.

If the researcher had been only a technician, no research into the worker would have occurred. This would mean a machine design with highest rates and probabilities of accidents. A minimally social dimension to the design suggests that the designer at least considers a laboratory or a workplace environment to investigate the worker. Assuming the worker is a human being means taking a look at the precise numbers and movements in a laboratory or perhaps the messy place of production. The more complete and comprehensive method of rigorous analysis includes two options: laboratory and workplace investigation. Taking time to examine the person's sensorimotor-memory when designing objects and ideas manifests the design's social nature, that the design is only for the user. Sociology and phenomenology converge as we find that design is a contextually constrained development, that productivity, competence, and functionalism are similarly restricted.

4. Our Design

When the technician designs a product with only mathematical and technical goals in mind, the design is a solely quantitative development. A design is only out-there; it is a discreet design apart from the equally discreet operator. Repeating the earlier statement, this is the Cartesian perspective as the object's design is itself an objectivism distinct from the subject or user. The technician looks at people only as mechanical things that will push, pull, turn, see, hear and do. Design is a solution to technical problems, never humanized. A society with such an attitude considers the machine as the sum total of things of which it is built, and never considers the consequences for its operator. But the Human Factors and phenomenological perspective show a design's communal foundations.

Human Factors experts designing a product see themselves related with and caring for all other people. We are all together, linked in chronological and in lived history. Those individuals include potential users. For these designers, Co-Being or intersubjectivity is the essential nature of each person. This intersubjectivity manifests itself most generally in social relations. Those relations are our daily interactions and community as we live with each other and acknowledge each other's humanity. However, technicians need to express themselves through designing things, and users need equipment properly designed for them by the technicians. Technicians need to design the object or, more accurately, the way in which the object interfaces or links with the operator, and the operator needs to work with an object.

Phenomenologically, technicians in Human Factors do more than just designing an object. They develop a product in light of their relationship with the user. Every technician is a co-user; as part of the user, as Co-Being, the designer is hurt if the user is harmed by a poor design. Every user is a co-designer; as part of the technician, as Co-Being, the operator ought to be part of the designer's efforts in building the equipment. Thus, the object or idea is fundamentally a reflection of the intersubjective nature of people, of technician and user. No machine or idea comes only from the technician's mind and hands. Each object is essentially growing out of the engineer's need to build objects for users and the operator's need for a tool. Designing an object means the technician and user are expressing their Co-Being through a technical enterprise. Engineers contribute scientific and technical competence, and operators contribute their limits and capabilities to orient that competence and professionalism.

Far from being a technical objective, the design is a communal product showing that at least two people helped build it for each one's sake. Engineers find satisfaction in making a design that will produce something when an operator operates it. Users find satisfaction in interfacing with a design that has been oriented around their sensorimotor-memory context. In this way, no machine or idea is ever designed for the sake of only functioning, doing, overcoming time and space in production. Every object and idea has been generated by people: designers want a career in which they are known for their ability to put nuts and bolts together and create a machine for production; but users want a machine whereby they can safely and comfortably work. Seeing the object's design, we see the technician's ability to develop raw material into a tool for themselves, and others. Additionally, we see the user having been allowed to influence the design so that any operation is more productive.

The phenomenological and Human Factors approaches put user-friendly objects into broad, cultural perspective. Just as individuals need nature and each other for existence and social relations, so they need to express their community in terms of building implements and tools together. A technician alone does not build the successful object. If that were the case, great harm would come quickly to civilization due to emotional and physical harm. Instead of engineers acting alone, they as co-users join the user as co-engineer and both of them, as Co-Being, design the object and idea whereby mechanical functions are realized as humanly oriented, socially desirable productivity. As technicians and users look at the design and the users use it, the engineers make the statement that they are technical professionals with certain competence, and the users make the statement that people need to use a machine to produce on their general terms. Without the engineers being able to research and design the object, and without the users being asked about themselves and their capabilities analyzed a community would soon wither and die. A community means, in part, people working together to produce kinds of goods and services that produce safety and comfort. Any society therefore comprises engineers who can and do grow by developing user-friendly objects because they assume the individual is a human being, and users (perhaps engineers themselves) who grow by feeling a sense of dignity and self-respect as they find their sensorimotor-memory needs acknowledged. We might argue that user-friendly design is the material or tangible manifestation of a broad social relationship. A phenomenologist would probably not argue against such a notion. The social context is not and cannot be divorced from its objects and thoughts.

When people meet outside, they may well relate to each other without objects. Yet, they may communicate eventually and thus use language. If they do so and no more within a building or other human-made structure, the user-friendly home or other building is the material context manifesting their social interrelations. If social relations enable individuals to express their intersubjectivity in a basic way, designing products is perhaps the most visible, tangible means of this Co-Being. We become ourselves in part by building human environments including objects and ideas that express our technical ability and the user's needs.

This is not to say that technique alone is an error. The technicians can err if they design something as only a technical problem and ignore the user: this makes the object only out-there, a discreet object-design to which to juxtapose the discreet user. In addition, the technicians can also do wrong by yielding to the user's unreasonable demands, fears, or other idiosyncrasies. In that case, the user demands a design that is only my design, and in that way takes safety too seriously. I can call this taking OSHA (Office of Safety and Health Administration) too seriously, making the environment so safe and conforming to the user's demands to the extent that the design is subjectivistic and virtually unfunctional. With only technical design, the user must make more effort than necessary to learn and adapt to the environment; this means emphasizing training and technology. At the other extreme, subjectivistic design overemphasizes design, whereby the user makes the least effort to function: this gets to the point where the human environment's function is too little to be productive.

In sum, a healthy society produces a reasonable amount of goods and services an amount not harmful to community and nature but also designs even this amount to be user-friendly. It does no good for a nation to produce higher amounts of goods and services with workers getting hurt or killed during the production process because of technicians or designers ignoring the user's limits and capabilities. Phenomenological cosmology rejects excarnating product design from the user. It reintroduces design into the user. That reintroduction assures the incarnate nature of design. Design is always design only *for* the user; the user is a user *of* design.

FOUR

AUTOMATION *FOR* USER

Chapter Three pointed out that design is ours and not just science and technology. Design must take the user's ability and needs into account. A fundamental ability and need is to be a user, and not to build machines that operate automatically. If each design of goods and services ought to be a design for the user's constraints instead of a technical development ignoring the user, then the product must itself be made so that the user will be part of the operation. The present chapter concerns a subset of user-friendly design: automation. A healthy nation requires a holistic attitude toward automation, toward machines that are united with an operator and not completely automatic. It makes no sense to have high production amounts when people are not involved in the production.

Books and texts in many different fields, from Human Factors engineering and management to the social sciences, and humanities, mention automation in terms of controversy. Experts debate the ethics and technical feasibility of increasing automation. Professionals are concerned with whether society will be able or ought to develop totally automated machines. Many researchers suggest that even if science and technology can build completely automated machines, a human operator may have to be nearby if not continually with the automated machine for technical reasons.

Increasing automation and the possibility of totally automated machines present a serious ethical issue for intersubjectivity. Co-Being argues that automation should be automation only for the operator. Applied phenomenology takes into account the view of many experts that technology may never attain the state of requiring no human intervention. Automation ought to be ours, and not only of the machine where motion is totally independent from the operator.

Whereas Cartesian dualism sees the subject-object debate only in nonethical terms, phenomenology and automation put it in ethical terms: machines without operators may be possible, but immoral. That fundamental unity between subject and object may mean total automation should not occur. Sophisticated systems will continue to require human operators because intersubjectivity is the context for and never distinct from objects.

1. Social Constraints: The Ancients

By definition, an automated machine functions in more and more ways by itself. This machine does things either that a human being previously had done or that a human being might never be able to do because of physical and other limits.. Ancient and modern society differ as to what people need to do.

Take ancient cultures. The ancients did everything according to the ways that their tribal gods, heroes, and ancestors had done in primordial time. The Maya, Native American, Inca, and similar people were among the ancients. Ancient communities put social cohesion and tradition above all else. Individuals had far less to do in early than in modern civilizations. They procreated and produced necessary food, clothing, and shelter. They performed acts in ways that perpetuated tradition. No action was only a technical event; everything manifested a social ceremony or reiteration of communal code. The were preliterate, oral communicators.

Ancient people's behavior was not as technique or physiology as is ours, but as ceremony. They maintained social cohesion instead of simply reaching a goal, doing, or performing procedures. With the goal of maintaining tradition, the ancients needed no innovation or more and more things to do. Thus, people basically were able to do as the ancestors did, because their objectives did not change overnight to thereby require sophisticated machinery and thinking about how to become more efficient.

In ancient society, human beings performed the functions and used simple tools. Individuals did these things in certain ways, the ways in which the gods had done them. No motion was only motion or going from point A to point B. Time and space were full, whole, and one; culture recognized the land as their land, their god's or ancestor's place. Individuals were to do something because of the manner in which it contributed to social goals, instead of merely to perform physical motions and be efficient. Ancient people believed in what we call social and ethical constraints on behavior. Activity was something for human beings, and for humans beings to do only in certain ways. Modern society practices such constraints to a point.

2. Some Modern Constraints

Modern society, pushing automation and efficiency, does practice some token kinds of ethical and organizational limits on technique. Not everything is only to get things done, and therefore doing so only mechanically. When police take a suspect into custody, soldiers die in war or accidents, or individuals perish in civil accidents and tragedies, officials usually refuse to release the names of victims or suspects before notifying the next of kin. Becoming a suspect in a crime, however minor, or a statistic in death, is serious occurrence. These have impact on the persons or their family and friends. Informing the press is more than conveying data; it is a social procedure and requires only certain people to be notified before the public learns through sensation and perception. Authorities inform next of kin before releasing names to the media. Gossip magazines and media could distort information about victims and suspects. Names are irreducible to data. Names belong to human beings.

Where national security is involved, the name of someone who may have been killed in the line of secret duty is perhaps never released to the public, and their work and means of death never acknowledged. National security generally transcends public information. The government ought never publicize or admit the existence of agencies vital to national security. Such control over what the media might say is important. What of allegations concerning control of media by big business? Researchers should take necessary action when learning of such control. They can inform the public and call for possible legal action.

However, society has, for good or ill, loosened constraints on certain events. Graduates may obtain their diplomas through the mail and graduate in absentia instead of being present with their class at the ceremony. Individuals in many contests are allowed to win many kinds of prizes without the need to be present during the drawing. A phone call or note is considered adequate, as winning means pulling the winners, names and automatically conveying information to them. Many people in modern society believe that living together automatically means they are in a relationship; they need not go through a marriage ceremony. In each of these cases, nothing is sacred about attending the graduation ceremony, being present at the drawing, or having a wedding. The goals are reduced to physical technique and motion.

If automation has not yet affected diet and marriage, it has found increasing use in work, education, art, and wisdom. Jobs and the learning process are the main places where culture introduces and expands the automated machine; art sees automation in ticket sales and payment. Presumably, wisdom is included in education.

From the perspective of modern society, people are doing so much more than in ancient cultures. Our food, clothing, shelter, and all else have become more in quantity, are sent to bigger markets at greater distances, and are more sophisticated. Individuals by themselves cannot construct a big building, provide heat and air conditioning to a city or even a building, acquire certain kinds of information from a library or other data bank. Machines are required and often need some automation. More and more things we have done, such as drive cars, planes, ships, and space vehicles become automated to make things easier, more efficient.

Motion and mechanization evolve into an objective apart from the operator. Building a machine seems to require only science and technology of motion and functioning. People need not do things, and society rarely asks whether those things we cannot perform ought to be performed at all. For example, ought there be nuclear plants, large construction projects, and so forth?

Alphonse Chapanis believes that we will probably never be able to build a fully-automated machine.[1] The issue of automaticity is not whether operators will be present at some point. The issue is the allocation of responsibilities between operator and so-called fully automated machines. Automation consists of two extremes, and a wide spectrum in between concerning such allocation. One extreme means the operators almost completely control the machine; the other means they are primarily concerned with monitoring, planning, and maintaining.

Usually, the fully automatic machine or system is the degree to which the operator has only the planning and monitoring functions. This implies that some systems would be totally without any operator. That might be wishful thinking. Phenomenologically, Human Factors in automation is expressing the inevitable. No machine or automation is a discrete, pure object to which society juxtaposes an equally discrete, pure operator. The deepest, most immediate level of experience, including the automation-operator experience, is the intentional unity of machine and operator from which the concepts of automation and operator are subsequently derived. Try as society may wish to, automation and operator are fundamentally simultaneous. The operator is given. While sensory deprivation experiments do not include automation-deprivation aspects, the fact that operators are always present in some form suggests that increasing automation continues to require the operator. The operator is an operator of automation; automation is only for the operator.

Barry F. Kantowitz and Robert D. Sorkin[2] oppose giving an operator unnecessary, meaningless chores. The operator probably should be present, but should do things that provide more than boring work. One point is that the allocation of chores ought to be given to an extent to the operators: they then have the option of performing tasks or allowing the machine to do so.

Just as intersubjectivity argues for the fundamental unity of subject and object, and thereby machine and operator, experts acknowledge the philosophical and implicitly phenomenological view concerning automation. At the most basic level, we see no clear and distinct manner in which to adapt automation. Society's views of machines, people, work, and its meaning of existence are the foundations of the kind and amount of automation. Hence, whether the future holds more, less, or the same amount of automation depends on what we believe about work, motion, time, space, and life. With the presence of operators almost guaranteed in every system, civilization itself may be the new sensory deprivation or operator-deprivation experiment: machines, automation, and people need each other and are fundamentally unified whether we like it or not.

Phenomenologically, allocating to the operator the task of deciding when to allocate responsibility may be a step toward giving the operator a meaningful task and bringing engineering and the automated system within the human being's control. Instead of someone else doing the allocating, the operators are able to do much of this themselves.

Machines are never totally reliable, and the operator may well be indispensable. Relating people to automation will no doubt be with us for the future. Jack A. Adams[3] appears to approach automation in a cautious manner. Automation is not monolithic. It depends on what people can and ought to do, and what machines therefore can and ought to do. Again, the operator is generally present, and society should not automatically automate everything. All of this also depends on what society believes people can and should do, and what goals and motions are beneficial to us. Civilization may believe that some individuals might be able to perform as cashiers, clerks and at other tasks without the need for automated systems. Would energy through solar power reduce the need for nuclear reactors and the automated problems they pose? For Shoshana Zuboff, the automation-operator web is a complex whole whose derived distinctions are to be carefully made, with more and more responsibility for such derivations put in the operator's hands.[4]

3. Social Factors

When, as I mentioned in the previous chapter, user-friendly design denies that systems are only technical, Cartesian dualism sees machine design starting from the technical aspect and ignoring the user's limits. The phenomenologically oriented automation engineer reintroduces design technology into the operator, thus beginning with the design and operator as a unity.

If design ought to begin with the social and psychological factors as well as technology, then increasing automation, which tends to ignore the operator, is Cartesian and at odds with user-friendly design's denial that design is technical. Emphasizing automation and only later wondering how best to bring in the operator is a technological perspective. Social factors are not meant to concern design alone; the human being does not disappear with automation. When automation begins with the purely technical perspective, it incorrectly assumes that the operator is not equally important.

Both bad and user-friendly designs assume that operators exist. When a design is unsafe and accidents occur, the Human Factors specialist can step in and redesign the machine to be user-friendly. The exclusively technical approach of bad or unsafe design still assumes an operator will use the machine. However, automation advocates and enthusiasts argue that we should start with automation as a technical issue, excarnate from any social and psychological context. The operators' role is not necessarily primary, equal, or simultaneous with the mechanization. Automation does not begin with social factors; it starts with what we can do with machines, and the goal to reach. Phenomenology cannot appreciate the overemphasis upon efficiency and speed. Personal relations, social understanding, and cultural enrichment are the basic goals for which the automated system is only a means.

To be successful, technicians must begin to reintroduce automation into the operator as a whole. A major need of persons, call it a limit or capability, is their basic unity with tools and goals. No individual can be deprived of machines; no machine can or should be deprived of the operator. Researchers sense that automation is deeper than science and technology. The phenomenologist Alfred Schutz says automation is ours, and irreducible to mechanization.[5]

When phenomenologists speak of the world as ours instead of mine, as intersubjective or social instead of subjectivistic and solipsistic, phenomenologically oriented automation researchers can interpret the phenomenologists in another way. Any automation is basically a manifestation of the technician or researcher and the machine and the operator. Thus, automated systems are, at bottom, ours. No automation can or should be the external machine, independent of the operator. Intersubjectivity means that any automated system is an *Umwelt* in terms of the *Mitwelt*; it cannot be only *Umwelt*. Excarnating the operator from the machine means alienation from the machine. Total automation suggests that persons and machines are two distinct entities, and that persons are alienated from the machine. Phenomenology and user-friendly design overcome our alienation from the machine.

Proper automation is a social goal. Engineers build the automation around an operator's needs and capabilities to work as such. People are arms, legs, social beings, Co-Being for a purpose: to engage in more than just monitoring or planning. Human beings must be as actively involved with a machine, even in automation, as possible. Seeing an automated system means seeing the engineer, technology, science, and the user. Taking away the last aspect may work for a while, but it fails in the long run because machines and people fundamentally are, or exist, before any artificial distinction and derivation.

To consider automation as a primarily quantitative, technological goal, as a physical surrounding or *Umwelt*, as an external objective excarnate from flesh and blood reality, is as wrong as design without user limits. No tool is entirely for the sake of performing an action; the developers make it for someone like themselves. Thus, the instrument is a mechanical means for a human being to accomplish a social, personal objective through personal engagement. Unsafe machines are not just those with designs posing danger to users, but are the increasingly automated systems putting speed and independence above the users. The belief that the users are less and less important reduces them and the machine to objects, where failure and social disruption can have serious consequences.

Increasingly unmanned machines deny the fact that people are, the world is, tools and instruments exist. They reject a holistic perspective that all things and people basically are interconnected. A convenient approach for the technician in automation is that the machine must be built, and that it is different or distinct from the social context.

4. Social Dislocation and Location

Beginning any automation project from the technological view means reducing machine and human being to objects. What is good business practice for increased profit can evolve into social problems and possibly disaster. If Human Factors engineers believe users ought be part of the project, and if other engineers assume individuals will be present (although they ignore their limits), automation engineers must assume that an operator will be present and have a reasonable, not caretaker, role.

Lived history is not far from the thoughts of many researchers in automation. For them, machines and systems are irreducible to science, business, and profit. Phenomenology, applied phenomenology, and intersubjectivity or Co-Being are making some headway, even if implicitly, into business and management systems involving automation.

Daniel Katz and Robert L. Kahn tell us that all too frequently, society presses on with automation first and seeks to fix resulting social dislocation thereafter.[6] Social dislocation implies social location, and both suggest geographical and philosophical meanings. When automation enters without regard for the human cost, people find themselves unemployed, moving to new locations for residence and jobs, and similar cultural problems. Derivatively, location indicates a person lives, works and plays in a place with reasonable job and other security. A town, city, or nation is the political-social-geographic context where individuals call themselves citizens. They are at home here. But seeing themselves part of the social context is derived from the fundamental location in a philosophical, phenomenological view. Location means persons enjoy dignity and worth, able to work for a living at a desirable job doing what they find satisfying. Society locates workers when they see them as irreducible to biology and chemistry, or less. Philosophically, location denotes the individual's connection with the past, present, and future: every individual is someone like us, a Co-Being for whom automation, if it exists, must include more than just superficial and observational status for the operator.

Philosophical and phenomenological dislocation consist of objectifying and reducing the person to a thing. Husserl warns us against fundamental dislocation when he tells us that individuals we meet are people like ourselves and not mere objects or anatomy. Phenomenological location is intersubjectivity, Co-Being. From the perspective of automation, it means developing automatic systems for the operator, where the operator performs important functions and has reasonable control over the machine. In such location, the operator is not distinct from the machine. A located person is continually involved with the machine. Phenomenological location results in geographical, political, and social location. But, phenomenological dislocation, reduction, or distortion of Co-Being result in social dislocation. As soon as society reduces individuals to an object, it dislocates them philosophically. In time, these people are replaced by increasing automation and are socially dislocated from one geographical place to another. Social location or dislocation are basically phenomenological location or dislocation. Thus, location is Co-Being, dislocation is reduction and Cartesian dualism. Social location enables the individual to proceed from fundamental Co-Being and toward derived national identity and citizenship, including geographical placement. Taking persons' job needs and abilities away from their Co-Being results in loss of Co-Being, loss of personal identity, and a sense of geographic placement.

Intersubjectivity sees location as the operator's place with machines. Person as operators are defined in part by their basic unity with machines, automated or not. This sense of fundamental or intersubjective location reintroduces the automation into the subject, so that an operator is never located by being a pure subject apart from a discrete machine. Phenomenological location is never solipsism or subjectivism; such location is always intersubjectivity and the subject-object, operator-automation unity. Any derivative distinction between operator and automatic machine is a derivative form of location. To start with the Cartesian view that a discrete operator is juxtaposed to the discrete automated machine is thereby a phenomenological dislocation. The dislocation makes the operator basically distinct from the automatic tool.

Researchers and scholars who argue for retaining the operator are pushing what phenomenologists, applied, and social phenomenologists call intentional unity between automation and operator, and what I call phenomenological location. Humanistic and social values indicate the nontechnological basis for work and profit; people are located as Co-Beings. Ignoring those values means operators are reduced to objectification.

5. Automation, Sequence, and Lived History

Automation concerns emphasis on sequences or serial motions without human involvement. Sequence in phenomenological perspective means *Historie*; the human perspective brings in *Geschichte*. When automation means justifying, expanding, and reifying sequences in order to increase efficiency regardless of human involvement, the engineers thereby look at *Historie* as more important than humanity. This is contrary to phenomenology, and other humanistic values. Sequence, and therefore automation as the sequences independent of people, can never be totally external. *Geschichte* is fundamental to *Historie*.

For Jack A. Adams, automation appears best[7] when dealing with work load, danger, or excess sequential operations that the operator cannot perform. Among these can be tasks involving nuclear reactors, major air conditioning and heating systems, prolonged repetition, tremendous information storage and retrieval, and physically heavy work. Automation is unnecessary for operations that a person can do well.

Take excess work load. Excessive work load means job situations in which workers have too many things to do and too little time in which to do them. Those in charge bring in automation in order to help the worker accomplish the overload. This sounds fair. Why burden the employee with too much work when, during certain periods of time, an automatic machine can step in and help? In this case, however, a philosophical question emerges. Should a job be analyzed to determine if periods of reasonable work load ought to be followed by times of too much work load? To assume that work load is work load, beyond our control, is to make a bad assumption. The phenomenological view explores the meaning of work, of work loads, of what people ought to do or produce. Intersubjectivity does not automatically believe that work is something external, and that we ought to justify excessive work loads and then bring in automation.

The company can reduce work load as such, instead of reducing work itself to the sum of operations and periods of varying load. If it is impossible to maintain a consistent level of work throughout the day, week, or month, a corporation may consider hiring extra, part-time help instead of reducing jobs to technical problems and then bringing in automation as a means of "solving the problem." Even if automation technically solves the problem of periodically heavy work loads, is there a deeper, phenomenological issue of the meaning of what culture is doing? Since people are performing effectively during regular work load periods, part-time workers, instead of machines, ought do the extra load.

Excess work load suggests people can perform some sequences but that other sequences become too much. From the intersubjective perspective, sequence is *Historie*, and demands something deeper. That something is intersubjectivity. It links past, present, and future: That something is *Geschichte*, or the involvement of human beings as groups, and analysis of the justification of the chronological sequence of events. This is closely related to Adams's point concerning excess sequential operations.[8]

Adams notes that automation can help when sequential operations are so great as to require more than the operator. But this can mean that culture justifies the sequential operations and seeks only to "solve the problem" by adding more technical means of doing the tasks. Where ancient society may have gone to one extreme in ignoring or rejecting tools for mechanical functions people cannot do, modern humanity may have gone to the opposite extreme: sequential operations are beneficial regardless of their quantity.

From the perspective of Co-Being, the meaning of work includes exploring the amount of sequential operations, things to do. Instead of accepting a quantity of large sequences requiring automation, a phenomenological view point begins by considering human beings and their existence. Phenomonology does not first reduce existence and jobs to sequence, procedure, or a series of times (each of which is a separate task). A lived analysis asks what it is that contemporary civilization is doing, what its values and institutions consider real.

Sequential operations and tasks cannot orient themselves. Serial motions are not their own justification and meaning. All procedures require something deeper and transcendent to historical time, as we shall see in detail in the final chapter. Automation benefits people primarily in the last resort when things to be done are too dangerous, physically heavy, or otherwise justifiably beyond human capacity and rights. Researchers in automation systems consistently look at *Historie*, and apparently rarely at *Geschichte*. *Geschichte* gives meaning to work load and can help determine if we need additional workers. It can help us see if the work is valid.

How individuals relate to each other, the past, the future, and the values and meanings that underlie civilization are immensely more basic than people's ability to do things or scientifically and technically solve problems. Work tasks are meaningful only in the context of existence or Co-Being.

Concentration on appropriate roles for automated machines, and human beings will continue to generate controversy. The technical Cartesian view is wrong to assume that the basic meaning of work involves sequences and operations as a discrete concept to which we then must somehow juxtapose the equally discrete idea of a human operator. To the extent that a culture begins with the reductive notion of mechanical functions different from human nature, people will continue to have difficulty in determining allocation of functions and responsibility between machines and operators.

Allocation of responsibilities is not the proper and orderly way to approach automation. Research attempts to see what people can do, and what they cannot or should not do. We then assign to the machine those things people cannot or should not do. Because allocation is derived and there is no clear and distinct difference between much of human and mechanical activity, assigning functions does not solve problems in automation. It becomes a matter of personal philosophy. In no instance is the automated system a given, distinct from the operator as another given. The given consists of the human-tool unity we call the broad context of civilization. Moreover, this tool is not reducible to a mechanical means that we can or ought to expand, or make more complex and intricate as desired. Simplicity and values are always basic. Only in cautious reflection is humanity to begin with the machine-person whole and then carefully derive ethical, socially responsible sequences and tasks requiring automation.

To begin by reducing people to what they can do best and assign other duties to something called a machine, totally distinct from human nature, only adds to our philosophical options and debate. Allocation of duties cannot inherently simplify technology and contribute to answering how and when to automate. With so many kinds of tasks and jobs, so many machines and combinations of tools, and so many differences or preferences possible in selecting when to automate, ethics and subjectivity more than technology determines automation. The Ricoeurian method is significant in that it tells us to reintroduce mechanization into civilization and meaning. In that sense, a culture will have to decide its goals, concepts of tasks and sequences, indeed the meaning of life or existence as a basis for determining when to automate.

From phenonenology's perspective, giving people the tasks of monitoring, planning, and maintaining automated systems, and giving automated systems the duties of performing sequences, seriously divides existence into the purely orienting and strictly oriented. Operators only orient, machines are only oriented. Luckily, this dualism is mainly an option, and is necessary apparently only in nearly unmanned systems. The oriented or chronological, however, is the oriented for the orienting. Co-Being means that the mechanical is for the human being, and the planned, monitored, or maintained for the planning, monitoring, or maintaining. Continual and serious perpetuation of the artificial, divisive difference between machine function and human existence results in more heated debate instead of significant, beneficial, and enlightening solutions of automation's problems.

Whereas Cartesian methodology begins with "I think, therefore I am," increasing automation often starts with "the machine can do, can perform as well or better than a human being, therefore the machine is producing when it does so automatically." But phenomenology has shown that objectivity is embodied and not disembodied. Objects are for consciousness and are not pure objects apart from discrete subjectivity. Thus, Co-Being argues that we objectify as existential beings; intersubjectivity therefore can say that the machine ought to perform something of an automated, sequential task within my planning, monitoring, and so forth. Phenomenology does not agree that the machine will do sequential tasks and I will stand back, orient, and perform nonmechanical tasks. Sequentiality and lived history are simultaneous: motion occurs within social contexts and cannot exist apart from culture.

Where Cartesian dualism is a nonethical, basically epistemological, or metaphysical view, automation brings ethical interpretation to the subject-object debate. The ethical notion is that object (automation) without the subject is not only metaphysically impossible, but also unethical even if it is possible for society to build an automated machine not requiring the operator.

If the experts disagree about the future consequences for employment of automation in manufacturing, and if various philosophies determine allocation of functions to what they perceive as two entities called people and machines, then automation experts will continue to have the problem of what to do with the operator, just as Cartesian dualism has the problem of relating subject to object. Most experts do not recognize the divisive nature of distinct machine and pure operator.

Engineering that considers the humanistic and social context may well point to what we can call the deeper automation. Such an attitude allows phenomenology to speak to technology and orient its meaning and purpose. If the Human Factors specialists relate to and learns from social and humanistic thinkers, they cannot help but acquire the notion of existential and ultimate meanings. Meaning is therefore not monolithic and can tell us that some jobs, that we think require a great deal of automation, can be greatly changed or perhaps eliminated. Meaningful work does not inherently suggest that if a machine's tasks are boring, those tasks should still exist and less boring jobs found for people. This puts the Sabbath above people; work and motion above human beings. In the true intersubjective sense, if we need automation and can replace the operator, culture should then rethink its food, clothing, shelter, energy, and other material goals. Should they be too complex, dangerous, boring, sequential, or in other respects appropriate only for the nearly unmanned machine, those goals or objectives may be meaningless. Primarily in instances such as space and interplanetary probes, where the unknown and danger are overwhelming, operators are eliminated. Yet, Kantowitz and Sorkin believe the human astronaut provides an adaptible, flexible means of solving unexpected problems.[9]

Given the unity of operator and machine, operator-deprivation for machines may be impossible, and, conversely, machine or mechanical-deprivation of operators seems equally incredible. The most automatic system appears to require at least an observer, the most cloistered operator seems to need manual, sequential, physical labor. A society that ignores ultimate and existential meanings and jumps headlong into increasing automation for the sake of productivity, efficiency, and quantity that society may attain none of those three in the long run. Paradigm shifts may well have to occur when a culture sees dangerous, boring, and laborious work and believes these are its only options along with automation. Nuclear weapons control and disarmament is one interesting example.

Instead of more nuclear weapons and the possible need to automate warnings about incoming projectiles, governments disarm. The foot soldier is always necessary on the battlefield, however computerized and automated the battle. Energy is another example. Solar power might make energy production less dangerous than nuclear plants.

If the transportation system appears to need more and more automatic signals, civilization can consider the amount and need for much of its travels. Why do people travel? Should they move around less? As I heard so often during the gas shortage of the seventies, is this trip necessary? In transportation as with so much else, the is too often becomes the ought. Automation is an expression of a culture which, seeing people do more and do as they should not, merely adds a tool to justify and try to correct things. Drivers during the early 1900s drove through Manhattan in New York to get from the East Side of New York to New Jersey. New York built the Verrazano Narrows Bridge to have autos bypass Manhattan, which has not abated the traffic problem. The region could have forced drivers to drive around Manhattan or provided mass transit throughout the East so that autos would not bring gridlock to Manhattan, especially when the drivers are not Manhattan residents. Bridges, metaphorical and physical, do not always work; as artifacts and expression, they are added symbols, and additiveness is not deeply meaningful.

Automation involves seeing functions to be performed, problems to be solved, then building machines to supposedly solve them, usually without human intervention. Philosophically, the automated tool is reducible to the assumption that when there is something to be done, we develop a technical means to do it instead of rethinking our values. That, for applied phenomenology and Co-Being, is superficial automation and mere engineering: culture needs greater, deeper engineering and automation.

If, as I indicated in Chapter Two, national and economic well-being is deeper than quantity of production, this certainly means something to the limits on automation. Intersubjective foundations of GDP denote social and ecological constraints on production amount. If automation is only to lead toward more production, then intersubjective constraints on production amount mean serious rethinking of the kinds and extent of automation.

The computer is indispensable to much automation. I have not mentioned computers for a basic reason, and I will consider them in the next chapter. I omitted mention of computers in this chapter because my basic aim was to show that automation ought to be inherently related to intersubjectivity. Automation is *for* intersubjectivity or Co-Being. We cannot begin by assuming that a discrete object exists called the automated machine, allocated with certain functions, to which we then juxtapose an equally discrete operator allocated with other functions. Therefore, I am not interested in detailing the physical constituents of the automated system: those aspects are irrelevant to our philosophical position. Chapter Five considers Co-Being and the computer as such, whether it is part of or aside from automation.

I submit that if phenomenology insists that no facts are outside being or context, then, phenomenologically, no motion, no automation, is outside being or context. Total automation may be technically impossible, because no object exists without subject. Total automation is unethical. The healthy nation produces with operators in reasonable control of machines, and does not seek total automation. It does no good if a nation produces ever greater amounts of goods through completely automated machines. Phenomenological cosmology as business rejects excarnating motion from the operator. Co-Being reintroduces motion into the operator, thus assuring the incarnate nature of motion. Mechanical motion is always automation only *for* the operator; the operator is an operator *of* automation.

FIVE

COMPUTING *FOR* SOCIETY

The computer is a modern invention. Having begun essentially as a machine to rapidly solve mathematical problems, it quickly evolved into a symbol-processing machine to do something else also as rapidly as possible: display intelligence. Civilization appears comfortable with what constitutes a number-cruncher. However, computer scientists, psychologists, philosophers, and others continue to debate the nature of intelligence. We are uncertain as to the meaning of thinking, reasoning, or being intelligent. But does society benefit by producing higher amounts of goods and services when this means defining and solving problems quickly, even if those problems are not beneficial? The healthy society defines and solves problems with human as well as computer methods, and always rethinks the nature of problems and computers.

Phenomenology can indicate the ethical and technical limits of the computer. What should computers do? What can they do? For Co-Being, the computer as a speedy machine must be ours, and never only the rapid problem-solver. As ours, the computer ought solve only problems that are both very large and justified, instead of just any large problem. Society docs not progress only by solving problem after problem in a serial fashion. Computers are not the problem-solving method, simply resolving something that we take to be a problem. Since they are ours instead of simply the method, we share with each other the ability to solve problems. With the computer we share only those functions making life easier for us: we ought not try to put human intelligence into the computer and signify that intelligence is reducible to the intelligence process.

Michael Heim's *Electric Language*[1] reflects on the philosophy of the word processor. The advent of the word processor dramatically changes life, especially knowledge and writing. Individuals can write and publish on their own. No longer are we restricted to a sense of place. We may produce print anywhere, and communicate from any place to which a laptop can go. Time is drastically cut as inventors and the public communicate with each other instantly, and receive immediate feedback. Is the word processor good? Is the computer good? However, the computer and any writing must be explored in terms of its relation to people. They may make our life easier, but we must decide if something ought be easier. Heim's book puts the person-computer, especially the person-word processor relation into focus. He says we must constantly think about the word-processor's capabilities. Heim advises us not to abandon this technology. He also warns us not to conclude that the computer and mind are the same in structure.

We should always rethink computers and their relation to us.

1. Cosmology, Religion, and Astrophysics

In Chapter One, I pointed out that cosmology was much broader and cultural than science. Cosmology is irreducible to astrophysics. To understand cosmology or the study of order, it was necessary to consider Co-Being, wonder, and awe that things *are* as basic elements of knowledge composing lived history. Lived history's classification in terms of disciplines constituted a derived form of Co-Being. Co-Being is compatible with reasonable objectivity. Phenomenologists would say that Co-Being and objectivity comprise a continuum.

The effort to find cosmos, order, or meaning was shown as humanity's very nature as a cultural effort. Cultures have searched for meaning or orientation since the dawn of time, they do so now, and they will continue doing so.

Humanity's earliest attempts to discover meaning were religious, and many people continue to look to religion for fundamental or ultimate meaning in existence. As Paul Davies[2] has commented, these earliest, religious cosmologies have a flaw that an intellectual finds difficult to accept. With roots in complex theology, revelation, and mysticism, early religious theories of existence reflected the local tribe's provincial world view and therefore were not uniform throughout the world. A theory of the universe must be uniform, because reality, existence, or the universe is one, regardless of the particular time and place. Phenomology, uniformity means intersubjectivity; all people share in it, and the theory reveals all individuals as part of each other.

Astrophysicists are pointing out that primitive civilizations' religious theories of existence have evolved into our astrophysics. We know that major religions continue and strive in many instances to reconcile modern astrophysics with traditional but growing spirituality. In other words, astrophysical cosmology attempts to do the same thing that early, spiritual cosmologies did and, in a sense, that contemporary religions proclaim: help us understand the meaning of existence. Astrophysics is seen to have a definite edge in that it performs its work with experimentation, intellectual and especially quantitative inquiry, rather than what some physicists believe is much spirituality's myopia due to tradition.

To be fair, however, we repeat that not all astrophysicists are materialists. True, their concerted efforts are toward a quantitative theory of existence bringing together the strong, weak, electromagnetic and gravitational forces. Yet, as astrophysicist Davies has indicated, various aspects of the new physics, including curved and expanding space and time warps, come over well for individuals with a religious and mystical bent.

Thus, what began with early religions and continues in a sense with modern religions has come to be astrophysics' claim to fame. The physicist tells us that nature is phenomena, and laws of nature are our fundamental intellectual goal. Now, however, computer scientists seem to be making the picture more complex.

2. Ancients, Astrophysics, and Computers

The phenomenological approach to computers is comparable to that of Joseph Weizenbaum. He believes that computers need ethical[3] and not just technical constraints to what computers can do. The problem restricted to a tiny circle of computer researchers is the deepest issue having concerned humanity since we can remember. Our basic question concerns existence: who are we, why are we, why is there anything rather than nothing? To many individuals, modern science apparently has the corner on the question, and perhaps the answer. But ancient religions promulgated cosmologies first. Where ancient people sought to see what our relationship was to deity, and that we had to wonder and be awed by God, modern science has sought to analyze humanity and see what type of scientific animal or machine the person is. Religion was once the center for such an issue. Now, modern science takes over. Yet, do we have at least two branches of the meaning of existence? If computer science and astrophysics each claim to be looking for the basic laws of existence, one in the person and the other in nature, each is similarly claiming that that set of laws and rules pertain to different areas.

Astrophysics says it inherited ancient religion's quest for meaning and now has the ability and duty to discern that coherence by finding laws of nature itself, the basic unity of the four forces external to people. Astrophysicists do not talk of computer science's goal of formalizing thought as equal to the laws of nature. Now, listen to computer science. Its experts are telling us that it inherited early religion's search for coherence to phenomena and thought, and it is the modern field of knowledge that can and should discover that theory of existence. Its domain, though, is not external nature; computer science seeks an answer to existence literally inside the brain. Unity of astrophysics' four forces as such means little to computer science's research for a formal set of laws of thought.

Do we see a neo-Cartesian dualism? Computer science seeks coherence of phenomena in terms of cognitive rules or how we think. A theory of existence concerns human intelligence: the subject. However, astrophysics claims such coherence is one of natural rules or what there is external to the individual: the object, in time, space, and matter as the four forces. If a set of laws explaining or even proving phenomena can exist, would it be strictly cognitive or only natural? Suppose astrophysics finds its unified field theory and explains the four forces; then imagine computer science coming up with a set of rules formalizing thought. It would be almost schizophrenic for intellectuals from two distinct fields each to claim finding the fundamental coherence to phenomena. Is there a nature apart from cognition? Probably not when a human being is finding and understanding that nature, unless we speak of the pure object. But that would mean a discrete object apart from the discrete individual. Can there be mere cognition without a set of laws of nature? Most likely not, for thinking means also thinking about natural laws.

To say nature or objectivity is inherently something other than cognition suggests having started from the divisive distinction between object and subject. The whole is primary. Thus, nature and astrophysical laws ought be part of any coherence and not exhaust the unity. We should reintroduce astrophysics into cognition as a whole. My first chapter points out a phenomenological approach to this. That chapter constitutes cosmos or order telling us the world is; it also shows classifications in lived history as a derivation from wonder. The remaining chapters, including the present one, flesh-out that derivation. Astrophysics and natural laws are meaningful within the first chapter's context, and the entire book is, in a sense, our cognitive-existential, humanistic context or view necessary for understanding nature.

Two things strike me as intriguing. If the universe ultimately includes us,[4] as Davies indicates, a unified field theory would be, at bottom, intimately interwoven with human cognitive effort. Indeed, such a comprehensive theory can only exist if it emerges from human experience as such, not just cognition. Scientists came to discover nature's laws. No nature, no natural laws made by individuals, can be totally external and unrelated to cognition.

The other item is that cognitive science thinks of astrophysics and science more than most astrophysicists acknowledge formalization of thought as equal to natural laws. Astrophysicists do not as a rule consider the psychological, or cognitive means of arriving at their equations; cognitive science does think about how a person thinks and arrives at a theory of existence.

3. Derivation, Computers, and Bias

Phenomenologists believe the act of deriving subject and object is most likely the fundamental level of computing, of objectifying and attempting to define and solve problems, of displaying intelligence. Co-Being or intersubjectivity is the basic bias or prejudiced orientation we call existence, within which derivation or fundamental computing occurs. I tend to call fundamental computing the kind of intelligence that people have or display by themselves, without the computer, that science makes. To derive subject and object is to compute, objectify, understand, and so forth. In other words, my first chapter reveals this derivation, or human computing, as I attempted to derive the notion of existence and analysis, and the rest of the chapter outlines this book. Through derivation, I pointed out a classification of disciplines composing lived history and indicated this book's direction. As a whole, the remaining chapters, including the present one, flesh-out my first chapter's nature as an isomorphy tying together different aspects of lived history.

The subtle bias in phenomenology is the intersubjectivity orienting and directing derivation. Speed is not important. Scientists do not need rapid thinking, especially with a computer, to develop ideas. Computers can and do help in solving many problems scientists have within the course of their experiments and theories. In the main, however, scientific research occurs with persons reading, writing, arguing, lecturing, and so on, all of which involves human activity going at the normal pace. Computers help along the way, but they do not develop the main themes. The computer as rapid machine becomes beneficial and indispensable when any area of knowledge confronts major calculating problems too big for the human mind. Computers for Co-Being mean that within derivation or human intelligence itself, the computational act should be less an effort to duplicate human derivation and wonder, and more a cautious, judicious computing of large problems ultimately helping humankind. No point is made of the notion that the computer must imitate the person. Formalization of thought is something that researchers most likely will never achieve, for no individual can really stand totally out of existence for an objective view of Co-Being. Derivation in terms of human intelligence is only that, rather than discovery of a formal set of logical rules basic to such human computation. Phenomenologists believe that computers are to help us with big problems and not to become like us.

How, then, does phenomenology reconcile a set of natural laws with a formal set of rules of thinking? For Co-Being, laws of nature are meaningful not in themselves as a distinct science, but within phenomenological and ethical constraints of context. That context can mean a context of contexts; for example, the string of ideas in my first chapter, and those underlying the other chapters. This is in line with our view that cosmology is irreducible to quantification. Computing itself is irreducible to logic, quantification, rationalism. Astrophysics is ultimately only for lived history.

Scientists *are* and their existence is a bias or orientation for their derivations, calculations, and intelligent procedures. Additionally, scientists follow certain lines of assumptions and not others. These lines are inevitable biases or prejudices directing the scientific outcome. For Jeremy Campbell[5] the completely open mind is a fiction, for it would be unable to set, strive for, or arrive at any goals. Such a mind probably lacks the orientation for a proper direction. Without a bias, all sorts of experiences, disinformation, misinformation and data would overwhelm it. Correct and incorrect bias exists.

Insistence on a purely objective nature mirrors the false bias or prejudice in the reality of an external world apart from the thinker. At the other extreme, a computer scientist who assumes that logic is unrelated to the world has a false bias, in cognition disconnected from objects and experience. The intersubjective bias is closest to reality; Co-Being assumes nature and society are one, that objectivity and cognition are embodied in the social nature of civilization. Nature, and social and intellectual diversity emerge through careful, biased, or contextually oriented derivation as deep computing. If phenomenologists would give a name to computing where we start with Co-Being and derive problems for rapid computation and intelligence, they might provide the term "deeper computing." Many computer science researchers see a depth in intelligence where deliberative, serial, objective, sequential (*Historie*?) emerges from the predeliberative (*Geschichte*?) or what I call Co-Being.

4. Predeliberative and Deliberative

Computing or intelligence in its deepest sense is derivation of subject and object from intersubjectivity. Intelligence or computing cannot be a purely externalized process that researchers can excarnate from existential and social involvement and delegate to a machine. The computing object is an object for involved individuals, never a cold machine that can duplicate our intelligence. In other words, intelligence or computing is ours, and not only the external, excarnate process. Computing as intelligence or deriving is a human being deriving. Only when it does things too dangerous, tedious, or difficult for us can it mean artificial intelligence.

How do individuals think? What is intelligence? Jeremy Campbell says many computer scientists now assume that persons think or are intelligent in terms of at least a twofold path: a predeliberative[6] or Co-Being context for the deliberative,[7] serial or derived thinking. Predeliberative thinking may well be our being, our Co-Being, the wonder that we exist, that the world is. It interacts with, and is the context for deliberative thinking where classification and codification enter.

Descartes would argue that the deliberative processes are by themselves and not embodied. His view would be that deliberative and predeliberative are two distinct substances, instead of deliberation or objectivity *for* the predeliberative. But the phenomenologist tells us that it is necessary to reintroduce the deliberative into the predeliberative. A human mind works with the predeliberative orienting the deliberative or serial, and therefore one must be careful not to assume that speed alone is the answer for developing computers to imitate our minds. No human brain works in terms of purely logical, serial, step-by-step operation. As of now, no machine has been able to duplicate human intelligence, because so much is unknown about it, and, it works through embodiment and not merely in serial steps or sequence.

The phenomenological view suggests that predeliberative thinking is *Geschichte*, orienting deliberative thought as *Historie*. Machines we are creating do not yet have in them lived history, and they may well never have if the human is a unique creature as embodied. Where derived thinking interacts with and is for Co-Being or predeliberation, divisive thinking is derivation without Co-Being: here we find pure object and subject at the start, and the effort to find knowledge strictly through serial, chronological solutions.

Taking deliberative thinking too seriously, or apart from Co-Being, usually assumes that any coherence is strictly classification we impose on phenomena, rather than the fundamental unity of intersubjectivity or wonder. That is, pure deliberation implies the human is a blank tablet dependent on experience for knowledge.

Classification is derivation of classes, diversity, and intellectual coherence from Co-Being as fundamental coherence or unity. We are; derivatively, the mind consists of a classification system making rational sense of perception. These derivations bring us the isomorphies that I suggest make up my first chapter and in part, this book. No individual wonders at or appreciates being or existence in deliberative terms. And this is even true of the deliberative classification or computation: that intellectual orientation emerges through complex human development and interaction with the world.

If computer science wishes to duplicate intelligence, it would have the task of understanding how (why?) an individual exists, wonders, or appreciates Co-Being, and then derivatively develops a mental classification structure that works within the existential, social contexts. If, as phenomenology argues, being is irreducible to logical rules, and even derived classification is based on or for the irreducible, it seems impossible that artificial intelligence can explicate our existence and categories. Proof starts with derivation and deliberate control over experience and extends to a subset within derivation, where speed and cold logic might rule. Our beliefs are debatable but not subject to analysis. Knowing and believing or assuming are fundamentally our being-among-others-in-the-world, and are only derivatively explicable. Contrary to Cartesian dualism, predeliberative and deliberative thinking are simultaneous.

5. Derivative or Divisive?

Derivative, deliberative, serial thinking interacts with predeliberative thinking and means being intelligent. Phenomenologists would speak about the predeliberative-deliberative continuum. Instead of Descartes's *cogito ergo sum*, this is the phenomenologist's *cogito ut sum* or "I think as an embodied being," mentioned in Chapter One. My being is that of an embodied and not disembodied intelligence. Embodiment is of the object, and the object is for embodiment. Derivation or computation is what any person does within the existential context, seeing a relatively discrete object from subject.

However, the computer we call a machine can help us by solving problems, and perhaps displaying intelligence, quickly. Most of our problems can be solved by the human being alone, many require speed. Given the need to solve many problems as fast as possible, it is probably not dangerous. Yet, these are still well within the intersect, to use mathematical or set theory terminology, involving being and derivation or computation for Co-Being. Speed and computers is a subset within the intersect, for it means quickness is a virtue to an extent. What happens with either mere being or derivation?

The most likely idea is that of set theory's exact set. A phenomenologist calls it divisiveness or dualism: the starting point in Cartesian dualism where there is discrete object and subject. Pushed to that point, being as an exact set may be solipsism, devoid of objective experience and social reality or Co-Being, while derivation, computation or objectivity as an exact set brings us to (positivism or) the mere machine and thinking reduced to logic. If, as phenomenologists argue, sensory-deprivation experiments prove that intersubjectivity cannot be apart from objectivity, divisiveness consists of building a machine to duplicate human intelligence without realizing the machine must interact with the world as we do. Such a machine does not know that it knows.

If, as phenomenology suggests, we know an individual is someone like us before any biological classification, this implies that only the individual we so encounter is capable of intelligence as are people. When I see a machine, I know it is not someone like me. For phenomenology, it is likely that a machine, which I immediately recognize as a something instead of a person, cannot therefore imitate human thought. Additionally, if such duplication and imitation are impossible, can we explicate them? Probably not, unless we fully understand the meaning of meaning, existence, and explication. Thus, to be satisfied with derivation, even speedy computing to a degree, computer scientists can pursue the lines of those who look into predeliberative, nonserial contexts for analytic thinking. As soon as this is unsatisfying and scientists wish to go further and formalize all thought and put it into a machine, they become divisive. Descartes had the problem of relating pure object and subject. Divisiveness will experience the problem of even building the formal system (in light of the difficulties of finding the formalism) and integrating it within human life's tragedies, inconsistencies, paradoxes, and ethical dilemmas. The difficulties scientists have in isolating the formal system's set of rules says something about their experiential, contextual nature: none are strictly external.

Building a formal system might well be impossible given the extent to which the inexplicable pervades life. To stand back fully and look at the rules implies that basic rules exist. More importantly, and incredibly, full explication has the problem of indicating how we can exist and not be able to fully explicate, and then exit from that existence into another existence from which to observe the first existence. Are there two existences? That is hardly likely. Assuming there are, for the sake of argument, why not then stand back from the second position to see the rule about explicating rules? That notion complicates and runs contrary to the need to economize in life.

If derivation is insufficient for analyzing Co-Being, the further position is not better analysis but divisiveness and isolation. Derivation and Co-Being are simultaneous; divisiveness suggests we can stand back from Co-Being totally, no deliberation for predeliberation. Two completely distinct existences, one from which the analyst observes purely objective rules and existence, is philosophically inconceivable. If thinkers exist and seek completely to analyze that existence, they must then "exist" when totally explicating the first existence. But then, existence and existence must mean the two have something in common: the fundamental Co-Being that is irreducible to objects. Individual cannot exist in two existences that are so different, yet are "existence."

Human and machine computation are always to be within the predeliberative, always only derived. Take the machine and strive to make it as intelligent as the person, and you are trying to imitate the predeliberative and nonserial through the serial. That is the reason parallel processing is better than serial processing. The parallel processor solves problems simultaneously, solving various parts of the problem at the same time. Divisive computing, totally artificial intelligence seeks the whole in terms of the parts, devoid of the awesome and asthetic. That is why artificial intelligence fails, for existence is as aesthetic as logical. Emphasis on speed or brute force alone reduces problems to serial thinking, thus robbing problem solving of the simultaneity it naturally requires with the intersubjective.

Predeliberation assumes existence is more than solving problems. Life is also play, coping, appreciating, loving, caring, changing our mind, and so forth. It is not fundamentally or always a challenge to resolve and resolve logically. For every problem to solve or obstacle to intellectually overcome, we need only remember that human beings also need festivals, love, belongingness, and so forth. Co-Being is fundamental and intersects with the set of derivation: problem and mystery slide into each other. Another way of putting it is to say that each moment concerns wonder and our involvement with each other, and this social nature underlies any problem that emerges. Most of these problems are no bigger than the human being can handle through human ability, some do become big enough to require speed and computers.

When problems are seen as too big, we can give them to the machines in the subset where speed is essential. These kinds of problems are not the only ones we have in society. If every problem is suddenly very big, something needs to be done about the society. In other words, issues that to grow topsey-turvey may well be divisive. Their parts are not interrelated aspects of a gestalt, but juxtapositions manifesting a divisive world-view. In a sense,

Phenomenology can analyze a problem and determine whether it is derivative or divisive. The divisive world-view reduces Co-Being to objects, data, and problems. Existence is reduced to a series of problems. Divisiveness says that we need computers and other technology to solve them. Divisive thinking never wonders that the world is at all: existence is departmentalized and never a whole. Divisiveness means that serial thinking is excarnate. Divisiveness rejects the notion that serial thinking needs a holistic context.

Derivative thinking does not reduce Co-Being to objects, data, and problems. Derivation involves wonder. We wonder that the world exists. Existence or Co-Being reveals itself through interconnected parts. From time to time, small problems emerge and we solve them without computers. From time to time large problems also emerge, and we need computers to solve them. Problem solving and serial thinking must occur in a holistic context irreducible to data.

It may be ultimately impossible to build a machine that can imitate human intelligence and solve our mathematical, to say nothing of social and philosophical problems. Those who say we can build such a machine assume that issues are only external. The assume that problems exist without human intervention and feeling. People define and solve problems through a bias, an orientation, and not lockstep thinking.

Derivation tells us to solve small problems without computers. Shopping, play, travel between home and work should be small problems. Large problems can include national and international communications, airline and rail schedules, academic research, and other complex issues. Some large problems can be solved without computing because these require social changes. Urbanized transportation is such a problem. Many people believe that work can be far from home. Work does not need to be near home. They say the problem is how to travel speedily between home and work. This is divisive thought. It solves the problem by building expressways and mass transit between long distances. Derivative thought says the distance is the problem. Building small cities where home is near work solves the problem.

6. Involvement as Basically Inexplicable

We will find it impossible to build a machine to imitate human thought, because each of us is Co-Being and derivation, with the conjunction suggesting organic unity instead of additiveness. More accurately, it means Co-Being-oriented-derivation. Derivation, logic, serial thinking unfolds from Co-Being's all-pervasive nature. Information or knowledge is not a discrete piece of data stored in a certain place and found through a specific, logical step. Information gradually emerges through interactions and mystery.

Knowledge as derivation is not something in a certain place. While the brain has particular influence on information, within the brain knowledge is everywhere, and within the body and social milieu, knowledge is, for various purposes, in all places and times. We cannot pinpoint information as here and not there. Thus, derived thinking cannot be totally objectified, isolated, experimentally reduced or duplicated in a speedy machine. Knowledge is interaction instead of a thing. Self-knowledge or awareness that we are Co-Being is even less a piece of data and more the wonder that things are, that I am, that beings exist. Thus, artificial intelligence cannot imitate derived or predeliberative knowledge or knowledge of the self. The self is a co-self and our involvement with beings in the world. We are to live and not just analyze the self. If information in the derived sense is not located in any particular place, certainly Co-Being as the foundations of derivation cannot be reduced to explicit knowledge. Divisive information as data may not exist. Jerome Bruner[8] has pointed out that knowledge or information is interaction, it is existential more than empirical. The system of classification, the mental structures we need for coherence, are themselves embodied in the self or Co-Being as the context of living. This is our being-in-the-world with its social and cultural customs, instead of rules to be put on the books or with which to simply lecture.

Since derivation or information is everywhere, Co-Being is fundamentally inexplicable in that it is this everywhereness as such. Our involvement in the world is the fact that each of us is essentially Co-Being, everywhere during every time. People are all places and times, as social, intersubjective beings. Such unity is the foundation of any logic, and therefore cannot be reduced to visible, intelligible rules to be put into a computer. We do not stand outside isness itself, since that assumes at least two kinds of isnesses. But isness simply is. Its explication as derivation is therefore restricted through living and being human.

When phenomenologically oriented computer experts speak of data as everywhere, they seem to say that information is interobjectivity instead of an object. That makes sense if individuals are intersubjective? Human beings are as Co-Being, intersubjective, none of us private and distinct from others. Derivation of subject and object reveals what appear to be objects, but an objectivity that is finally interobjectivity. No individual, no logic can ever know or isolate the objects, because there is at least the (derived) context of interobjectivity. And no method can ever fully disclose or objectify what is clearly not an object: fundamental context of intersubjectivity or the self.

To recall Heim,[9] the computer and word processor may be compelling us to think about our relation to machines. We cannot abandon the word processor as destroying subjectivity, or embrace it with all our strength for making life easier. If electronic print harms community, we must rethink the extent to which people can allow themselves to use this invention. If electronic language helps business, education, and other institutions serve the neighborhood, person, and society better, then let us find those ways. Overexcitement about an innovation is as dangerous as underexcitement. We must reintroduce the electronic tongue into a social context to see what human activity ought be made different, easier, or more efficient. Naive acceptance of computers and word processors can result in excarnate thought.

7. Blurring Ethics and Technology

Can computers ever imitate human intelligence? Ought they? What I have just mentioned denotes the probability that researchers cannot duplicate what human beings can do. This involves the phenomenological view according to Stuart E. Dreyfus and Hubert L. Dreyfus.[10] They point out technical limit on computer speed. No data can exist without bias. Another view is what we saw in Weizenbaum. He argues that, while this may be true, we ought not even try to imitate human intelligence, because this ability is reserved for people.

I tend to see merit in both views. First, my entire argument in the present volume is to show that Co-Being is the context or fundamental unity for deriving subject and object, the classifications composing lived history's disciplines, all the chapters. Within each chapter, Co-Being consistently appears in a derived or applied form as the pattern or context for each technical, social, economic, and political situation. I concur that disembodied logic or intelligence is most likely impossible.

Hermeneutics shows that a logical or formal set of rules most probably could not exist, for a text or any sentence is not referring to something outside the reader, but a relationship between reader, author, and interpreter. No world exists outside the human being. Therefore, astrophysics is only for the participant and part of lived history, and a unified field theory must include human involvement, including phenomenological research. Thus, no purely logical sentences devoid of the reader's relation to the text, author, and others exist. Arificial intelligence may be impossible for individuals bring their own meanings and prejudices to the text, and interrelates with the author's biases.

Individuals are more than logical, mental, or sensorimotor technicians. They are embodied, ethnic, geographical, social citizens colored by every conceivable facet of life. No technician exists without value, life-style, character, or other human characteristic. Stewart and Mickunas[11] note that the society that isolates technician (what I do) from value (who I am) can cause peril, for persons are wholes rather than mental activity or technical competence.

Let me give an example. Imagine American and Russian (perhaps other former Soviet) leaders negotiating arms reduction. Both groups have to be technically competent. A summit without each side knowing about nuclear weapons, the laws, precedents, and political and socioeconomic milieu would be a disaster.

Members of both teams are technicians. However, they must be something more if they are to succeed as human beings, as government officials.

Individuals must know their own and perhaps the other's language.. A nuclear treaty exists only because individuals signed and wrote it in a natural language. The treaty does not drop from the sky or create itself. No discussion can take place without etiquette, protocol, tradition, embodiment. Nuclear arms are arms for human nationalities, and not things in themselves. Members of each team are technicians oriented in terms of personal and national identity.

Technician and being are inseparable, for the former derives from the latter. Since people are thinkers incarnate, thinking cannot become reduced to mere intelligence on paper. Mind is irreducible to a machine. Look into the brain to see the mind; look and relate to the body and society to see mentality. Government leaders and their assistants attending summits are American, Russian, and other nationalities instead of excarnate technicians.

Any intelligence is *ours*, and not just logic. Ethnicity is an interwoven web of connections so that every technician is a human being whose background is ultimately influenced by all other ethnic groups. When computers as rapid machines are used, such use and capacity is limited to what it can do, always at our mercy, never imitating and interrelating with us as an equal. Computers are *for* Co-Being in the sense that they are phenomenologically limited as to what they can do; they cannot be a duplicate of human intelligence externalized from people. There are philosophical constraints to objectifying thought.

But what of computers in existence? Does the view about ethical constraints for computing remain valid? Can computing for Co-Being also mean that existing computers ought be used only for socially and philosophically desirable problems? Should a nation's well-being include defining and solving problems because we can? Is the sum total of computer-solved problems, necessarily indicative of social benefit? Phenomenologists would emphasize ethics over the technical ability to solve problems. Phenomenologically, society should always rethink whether humanity is better off because it can and does solve big or small problems through computers. If, as many computer scientists argue, non-serial thinking is basic to serial thinking, then the sum of problems solved by computers does not indicate scientific and social progress. Even if civilization serially solves problem after problem with computers, this does not mean it advances. People could have solved the problems, assuming the issues were sound. If they were not legitimate problems and society considers itself having done correctly by solving them with computers (or even with humans alone), then legitimating and solving each becomes unethical. The computers existence does not mean we ought to do as we please with them. Let us not objectify or derive any more than we should.

Adding and subtracting without serious rethinking is computing for its own sake, objects for their own ends. Computing for the sake of computing is merely the solving of one problem after another, the serial solving of problems even if each problem consists of predeliberative elements. That kind of computing is unethical.

Intersubjectivity views solutions as *ours*. Phenomenology says values are simultaneous with problems. Values orient problems. Positivism or divisiveness says existence is a series of problems without wonder, and problem solving is an index of a nation's health.

Therefore, both ethical and technical limits are correct. The issue is not either ethics or just technology. Computing for Co-Being basically means ethics are involved. Do not compute problems that people can solve without a computer. Do not just define and solve problems even by human ability, because not all problems are valid problems. Co-Being also means that the computer cannot compute some problems because only people can live, understand, and solve them.

The healthy society takes a holistic view of calculation. People can use their own abilities to calculate and only at certain times resort to the mechanical computer for speed. Defining and solving problems is not fundamental to life; doing so within the context of intersubjectivity and wonder is most important. Existence is irreducible to problems and solutions. Society does not benefit by producing increasing amounts of goods and services when it reduces existence to serial thinking in people or computers, or worst, to the serial defining and solving through even predeliberative methods in computers. Solving problems does no good if these are not legitimate problems. Computing is only *for* Co-Being; Co-Being is Co-Being *of* computing.

SIX

INFORMATION *FOR* MANUFACTURING

The idea of the information or service economy takes too seriously the notion that knowledge is power. Acknowledging the power of knowledge means acknowledging that knowing means controlling our destiny and perhaps the destiny of others. People who lack knowledge, who do not know, are powerless. They are at least less powerful than those with knowledge.

If knowing suggests power, then Descartes's method presents us with the most fundamental road toward knowledge and power. Descartes indicates that his thinking means that he exists. Taking that one step further, I can argue that I think or know, therefore I am the most powerful. But the drawback soon becomes evident. Cartesian dualism separated thinking and knowing from embodiment. From the Cartesian perspective, power would be disembodied power seeking a relationship with existence or body. From the perspective of phenomenology, knowledge and theory must be *for* the body, Co-Being. What implication does this have for the purely information society?

1. The Disembodied Economy

Daniel Bell says that in the purely service economy[1] society puts knowledge or theory above manufacturing. Society has developed theoretical capability to the point where its professional intellectuals are able to compute their way toward the future. They have apparently found the certainty which Descartes so valiantly sought. However, if, as I argued, computers cannot control us (since they are at least ethically if not technically limited), then this presents a problem for the information society. Such a society, denying the equality of manufacturing and intellectual work, becomes unethical even if possible.

A service economy is the economic and social version of Cartesian dualism. Its philosophy is that of the disembodied information economy. The most prestigious occupations in such an economy deal with theory, computers, and knowledge. Manufacturing enjoys no prestige. However, people still need food, clothing, shelter, and other forms of security in manufactured items. Information is information only for manufacturing, for the intersubjective. Lester C. Thurow[2] tells us that many service industries exist to serve manufacturing.

Emptying manufacturing of its informational content and relegating it to less sophisticated, less allegedly powerful countries, does not take away the fact that the service society needs manufactured goods. Now, producing only information, the service economy becomes like the people trapped in a war zone: it must import all manufactured items in order to survive. For the phenomenologist, this implies an erroneous means of developing a healthy society. What good is it for a society to be powerful by knowing, when it becomes completely dependent on others for manufactured goods? The healthy society takes care of itself; it produces information but also produces by manufacturing.

By assuming that information and manufacturing are two distinct enterprises, the information society separates the cognitive and bodily aspects of a unified existence. Because work in a service economy is strictly information, the producer is reduced to a developer, transmitter, and receiver of data. The hands and legs serve only our cognitive capabilities instead of, for example, building roads, buildings, cars, trains, furniture, clothing, home and office equipment, and other goods. Knowledge workers work exclusively with knowledge processes instead of constructing things by hand.

The knowledge society develops theory and works with computers to control and manipulate the future. Such an economy reduces itself and humanity, to discrete bits of data, and mathematical formulas. But this reminds me of the astrophysicists' claim that cosmology is only quantitative. Mathematics alone cannot explain existence. A theory of humanity or existence must be the fundamental cosmology that takes phenomenological thinking as its foundations. Because such a theory is objectification, and objectivity is *for* the subject, the subject is manual and bodily as well as cognitive. Thus, a theory of existence ought to assume the importance of manufacturing as well as information.

The implications of putting manufacturing in a country other than the service-oriented society are philosophically and politically troublesome. I mentioned that the philosophy would be akin to a new Cartesian dualism. That view alone forces us to think of human nature as objectifying (information) and subjectivity (body, manufacturing). Phenomenology attempts to overcome this by insisting that we are both thinkers and doers; we think in terms of embodiment. The political ramifications are just as bad.

A service economy becomes the prestigious place to be. What of the people living in a nation that manufactures? They appear to become second-class humans, if that. These individuals are made to feel that their society is capable only of manufacturing, instead of thinking. Thus, their best and brightest students would necessarily consider work by hand as beneath human dignity and consider moving to the more sophisticated society where manufacturing is held in the lowest esteem. What a brain-drain! The philosophy of the service economy therefore tends to point toward a new colonialism, neo-racism and what I could term a jobism, occupationalism, or a professionalism where I consider the term profession as an ism to be avoided. The only professional is the thinker; the laborer is a lesser human being or worker.

If the service economy reduces uncertainties and increases its control over its own destiny and the destiny of others, might it not then seek to be the one superpower in a drastic sense? A colonial world results as the information superpower is more than a political power. It is more or less the superpower with superior people looking at others—manufacturers—as inferior. The logical conclusion of this outlook might be that knowledge workers are the only ones with insight into life. The manufacturers, since they do not know, are therefore controlled and manipulated by informed professionals as masters. This brings us back to the master-slave relationship.

The question then might be whether people in the service society encourage individuals of manufacturing societies to rise above manufacturing and toward knowledge work? We assume that individuals want to improve their role and position in life. With that in mind, it is possible that a manufacturing nation wants to change toward a service economy. They build universities and think tanks in their previously manufacturing societies. Would they be economically and culturally capable? What would an established service economy say? If a service economy nation sees its manufacturing source turn away from production, would we see a potential international incident? A manufacturing nation becomes transformed into the knowledge industry. Who manufactures after people no longer build things with their hands? The robot may manufacture. The dominant group, most likely the service or information economy's people, may want to force the manufacturing people to exist in their own notch. War could result. If the dominant group allows manufacturing peoples to change toward information jobs, then more nations change toward the service sector, with the remaining manufacturing countries being seen as primitive or third world. If manufacturing is inherently inferior, who manufactures after all nations turn to service economies?

Consider that every nation becomes a thinking, information society. This may sound hypothetical, but simply envision a world turning away from manufacturing, and look at what would happen after, say, a few hundred years. Everyone is part of a knowledge world; every nation does information. They still need shelter, food, clothing. So, we bring in robots.

But where do we put them? Perhaps we install them in the last nation that had been in manufacturing. The robots do the dirty, less civilized work, while every person does information work. Again, I am being hypothetical, since some people like to work with their hands. Assume we had sufficient robots working to manufacture everything that people around the world need. This may not be impossible if we do not have enough speedy robots and enough repairpersons, assuming the robots are not self-repairing.

In order to distribute the goods manufactured in this way, and unless robots are in each country, the seas, air, and land become trade routes as the world has never known. Anything we need that is manufactured must be done by robots, possibly in a nation or two away. The slightest accident, delay, misfortune or whatever with the robots would cause a serious problem of not getting the manufactured product to its destination. Imagine the logistics of determining, probably by computer, what is to be made and sent where. Phenomenology presents the easier solution: integrate manufacturing with service so that every city and neighborhood in the world has both information and manufacturing jobs.

Every nation would have both information and manufacturing professions, with neither aspect of life degraded. If society pays information people more than manufacturing people, it should equalize earnings for both sectors. Cartesian dualism is a spatial distinction, separating objectivity there from subjectivity here. The trend toward a service economy carries that to a truly spatial separation on a global scale. Service or information economies are certain places, as it were, while manufacturing nations the other places. Assuming the best intentions of humanity, intellectuals in the information societies will eventually help people in manufacturing nations to grow out of their inferior kind of work. Presumably, places where robots do their work are those with which one does not wish to be associated. They are ghettos where mechanical labor is considered something lower than human activity.

Cartesian dualism had to acknowledge the need for unity, and it would not be surprising if the most informed intellectuals ultimately saw the light concerning physical relations between manufacturing and service societies. I have mentioned the logistics involved in transporting manufactured goods from origin to destination. That means people, even the most expert theoreticians, need material or manufactured goods. Why separate necessary aspects of life? If subject and object are inherently intersubjective and we need to reintroduce objects into intersubjectivity, the economic implication is clear. Objectifying or thinking must be reintroduced into labor and manufacturing. It makes no sense to isolate aspects of a community and therefore to make a global separatism requiring extra shipping, handling, and freight to accomplish what an adequately prepared community can do.

Phenomenology brings unity into the picture of fragmentation, whether positivism or Cartesian dualism. It does so by sensing that mental activity is inherently incarnate, embodied, contextual. Where Co-Being enables one to see the error of positivism's discrete atoms, or Cartesianism's subject-object dualism, the economic interpretation allows one to conclude that a world divided into service and manufacturing places is wrong. This separation may at most be within the community. A city can have manufacturing plants somewhat far from information and service corporations. Even here, however, the distance ought not to be great. Thus, on the worldwide scale, no nation should be only service while another is purely manufacturing.

Chapter Two criticized a nation producing greater amounts of products and services while workers traveled long distances to work and indeed felt great personal distances in terms of being ignorant of clients and nature's needs. Indeed, each chapter of this volume is a critique of distance. One aspect of that criticism is to refute the physical distances between manufacturing and knowledge work. We can understand that this distance exists to the extent that various buildings in a neighborhood house different jobs. The same building or floor obviously need not be the location for both information and manufacturing. However, as spaces become greater and we think of the national and international scales, a given nation, indeed a given city or neighborhood can and ought to have both types of work.

2. The Possible Career and Family Crises

If knowledge is power and individuals with this ability take it too seriously, the next class or social structure can be foreseen as that between intellectuals and laborers. The worst-case scenario can mean devastation to both classes, not just the manufacturers. How many information professionals will force their children gifted or seriously interested in working with their hands to join the intellectual elite? Not every individual from a professional intellectual family is destined to follow in their parents' footsteps. A nation will continue to need maintenance engineers, painters, cooks, landscape designers, computer manufacturers, and so forth. Try telling the Big Three auto makers that their future is doomed as a prestigious type of work.

The anti-phenomenological attitude of intellectual parents, indeed the nation, could well be either to force their children to hate manufacturing or to disown them and move them to a manufacturing nation. That might be the easy part. What of ethnic and religious hatreds becoming manifest through a bigger crisis? A family might have it easy to compel, persuade or otherwise orient their child toward the politically correct information job. But given the world's cultural diversity, it is likely that certain people will use military and other force if necessary to oblige those they do not like to do the manufacturing. The world has millions of people who may have no choice but to do as they are told. In this case, the information professional's child is told to learn knowledge work, and the different ethnic group's or religion's child is directed toward manufacturing.

Word can get around that opportunity lies only in the service economy. Imagine millions of poor individuals in a nation with only manufacturing either rebelling or attempting to move to the more affluent nations. What do the sophisticated nations then do? Some could impose border patrols and threaten violence, making the Iron Curtain seem like it never came down. International tensions would certainly not decrease if, say, an information society suggests that citizens of manufacturing countries stay in their places. What an opportunity this presents for possible future terrorism, international hijackings, confrontations, and clashes with the notion that diversity is indeed part of life whether we like it or not.

A United Nations organization would have unprecedented headaches in a world in which the intellectual and manufacturing are separated, with prestige attached to the former and prejudicial implications emerging throughout nations. If a nation of intellectuals is better, more advanced, or otherwise more desirable than a manufacturing nation, and the latter seems to have no future, its leaders and forces might eventually decide that war is preferable to peace. Are the manufacturing nation's leaders intellectuals? If so, do they side with the professionals of the information society? This could lead to unspeakable social disaster for the manufacturing nation, perhaps even for the manufacturing nation's leaders, who could become targets for those they may be trying to keep down.

Phenomenology tells us it does no good for a nation to produce greater amounts of services if that nation does no manufacturing. Increased information quantity cannot improve a nation. Greater theoretical developments do not enhance an existence that degrades manufacturing. The world grows more unfair and unsafe with the subject-object dualism writ large in terms of manufacturing and information nations.

A healthy economy sees both manufacturing and information within its borders: each community reintroduces information within the context of manufacturing and dignity of appropriate manual labor. The enlightened thinker understands that these two are necessary aspects of a healthy person, and indeed a healthy nation.

Information is *for* manufacturing, and manufacturing is *of* information. Manufacturing concerns the body and means the hands and body in general cannot be ignored as a context or direction; information is cognitive, objectifying, reducing, and analytic, indicating that thinking is part of every manufacturing and nonmanufacturing person. The informed person is still a person; the manufacturer can still think. A society's manufacturing enables the embodying infrastructure to support, orient, and be the physical context for service and information.

National well-being depends on integrating information and manufacturing. A nation does not benefit by high production if that is only the production of information, and when all its manufactured products are imported. If it produces only information and when it imports all its manufactured products. Service and information are *for* manufacturing; manufacturing is only *of* service and information.

SEVEN

TAXATION *FOR* SOCIETY

If, as I have argued, cosmos is irreducible to astrophysics, national and economic well-being to production amount, product design to technology, automation to external motions, computers to serial thinking, existence to problems, and an economy to science, then what of taxes?

Readers may wonder what relevance a chapter about taxes has for the core curriculum? The answer is subtle. If lived history is basic to a core curriculum, and economic situations are part of lived history, then taxes, being an aspect of economics, are not far behind. I do not imply that the core curriculum includes detailed knowledge of taxation. Instead, I suggest that taxes are fundamental to jobs in two general ways. First, the worker and boss want less taxes from their pay; higher taxes mean a financial burden for the person receiving pay.

Second, more deeply, getting paid implies having a job as such. Higher taxes can discourage existence of jobs, while lower taxes encourage employment opportunity. It does little good for the worker to know basic skills and concepts of lived history underlying any given occupation when a tax situation may force jobs to move away, or at least bring down pay. Just as people need to understand the impact of technology, politics, cultural changes, and so forth on work, workers need also to reflect on taxation's implications for jobs and salaries. In short, taxation is not indifferent to work. Tax levels mirror society views about existence, problems, and money.

Co-Being denotes that existence is irreducible to money, and taxes are irreducible to the kind and amount of dollars and cents. Taxes must be *ours*, instead of more external amounts bureaucratically taken from a payer and given to a recipient. Intersubjectivity shows the social foundations of taxation: taxes are money to be taken from the payer only in limited situations and provided to the recepient only in light of a restricted social context.

1. Learning

Educators show us basically three ideas about learning or knowledge. These concepts can help us understand taxation. In the learning process, the student may be seen as actively interrelating with the instructor, passively receiving data, or actively able to learn without schooling.

First, Co-Being considers the teacher and student as learning together. They become co-learners. Students are inherently active but require proper guidance, direction, motivation, and data for their desire to learn. Instructors help students develop, treating each pupil as someone like themselves, a human being capable of growing and maturing. All instruction is part of a context in which the teacher and student are interpersonally involved.

Thus, learning is *ours*, a shared experience where teachers are changing along with the pupil, enabling the pupil to find out about both of them and become more mature and educated in values. Teachers do not impose external structures upon the students or allow the students to learn on their own. Learning is not the objectivistic process and content devoid of student participation. It is also not subjectivistic experience of the student lacking social context.

Our learning is akin to user-friendly design and phenomenology, where we design learning to take the individual into account. This kind of education sees the person's abilities and limits.

Second, the teacher must not impose an external structure upon the student. User-friendly design and phenomenology refute the notion that the learner is reducible to a machine. Objectivistic learning means the teacher knows everything, has knowledge, and stuffs discreet data into the passive student's sensorimotor functions. Learning becomes reducible to the sum of data, actions, and behavior. An instructor literally transmits knowledge, and the passive pupil receives this reductionist or atomistic amount of data.

We see the banking idea of education here, which Paulo Freire criticizes as dehumanizing. For Freire,[1] incompetent teachers believe they know, and the student does not know. The teacher deposits data into the empty student in order that the pupil have knowledge. Bad, unloving teachers give sums of data and instructions to students, as customers put sums of money into the empty bank.

Third, at the other extreme, subjectivism is akin to permissiveness. User-friendly design and phenomenology refute the notion that persons may learn as they please. We cannot design for the individual and require no effort on the individual's part. Subjectivism says, that students are active, and must never be taught, guided, or directed. They are on their own to learn through experience and assimilation.

Let us consider taxation in terms of social (intersubjective), socialistic (objectivistic), and anarchic (subjectivistic) society.

2. Our Taxation: Husserl, Schutz, and Ricoeur

Co-Being, intersubjective, or social taxation means society begins by seeing all individuals as people like myself. Individuals are part of each other, of me: they are Co-Being. The phenomenological perspective concurs with Elliot Richardson[2] seeking to show that individuals are all part of a social structure in which the state is good but must take freedom and liberty into account. Phenomenologically, the responsibility to help another occurs within the context of persons' rights to retain a respectable amount of their earnings.

For Co-Being, the political implications suggest we are all together as co-citizens. I have rights and responsibilities, not just rights or just duties. Each individual is inherently capable of doing things themselves, participating in society, and earning a living. The state can provide the opportunity to allow people to live in peace, but it should not mechanically direct redistribution of wealth. Persons are generally irreducible to money, existence is more than the sum of problems, and problems are not automatically due to the lack of money. Phenomenology means we must reintroduce redistribution of wealth into the freedom to retain over half of our earnings. The phenomenological approach rejects two extremes in the redistribution of wealth. One is the positivist extreme, where existence is totally reducible to wealth, and the state mechanically takes virtually all, of your earnings, so that almost everything is free.

The other extreme is the complete lack of any redistribution. If taxation is necessary, redistribution must occur. The libertarian extreme means virtually no redistribution of wealth, and the earner keeps almost every penny earned.

In my ideal society, redistribution is an objectivity within the social context where persons can keep most of their pay. This is a form of democracy. Total or nearly complete redistribution is centralization instead of democracy because centralization takes away most of a worker's earnings and other rights. Blanket or nearly total rejection of redistribution is anarchy and not democracy, because a state that allows earners to keep virtually all they earn, will never be able to insist on social responsibility. Democracy must insist on social duty, and reasonable redistribution of wealth.

To be one with other people denotes each individual's awareness that all citizens are defined in terms of each other. I am responsible to others in that I must help them see themselves as capable of self-government and problem solving. Each has dignity, and my duty to them is to enable each to see that dignity, freedom and self-reliance constitutes this participatory nature. That is, each citizen is a co-participant in society, doing for themselves and others. As social beings, persons belong to, receive from, and contribute toward intersubjectivity by being and becoming with all others. Persons gain identity through each other and share a common communal relationship as the basis of existence. I must help materially, but within the social context.

Existence reveals that each person's being, interconnected with that of others, is irreducible to problem solving, money, or material gain. Being with each other is more than an economic concept; it is fundamentally a social, interpersonal relationship in which our identities grow, mature, and develop. This is a cultural process and not an exchange of goods and services as such, requiring money and taxes.

Within the social context, persons may rightfully retain over half of their earnings without having a state mechanically, bureaucratically take more and more of this in taxation. The exact amount of taxation for a given person is beyond this volume's scope. I might say phenomenology would reject the simplist nature of a flat tax. President Ronald Reagan said government is the problem. Society's and any person's problems and needs cannot be reduced to money. Persons are never only a source for public funds. Tax recipients are never only receivers of such wealth. Persons have rights and responsibilities. Phenomenologically, we must reintroduce tax paying and receiving into social responsibility. The egalitarian is wrong in saying that money can solve all problems. However, the libertarian is wrong in saying that money solves little or nothing.

Rights denote liberty. Rights also mean my interrelated duty to materially and personally help others. I help them become themselves, but aid materially when they need these resources. I am free to keep most of what I earn or otherwise have saved or inherited. My Co-Being means first of all that people and I are together, and our unity is based on our being human and needing each other as persons instead of money givers and receivers. I will give money within the social context. What are my responsibilities? Phenomenologically, my duty is maintaining my security and arguing to keep that safe context.

But related to this is my duty to help others see their rights to keep much of their money and property, their dignity, and that of their loved ones. I am not Hobbesian. My security is related to the other's welfare. My duty therefore means I tell others that they must realize and develop their identities, beings, and capabilities in light of their social nature. Yet, I can help and not ignore them materially in this process. We are one; they must do as much as possible, as I do. I can help them accomplish this social goal. My duty to myself and the other includes both voluntarily giving money and other material resources, and allowing the state to redistribute a small but necessary amount of my income to the other.

My relationship to others is akin to a teachers' role with students. As I meet others, I help them see more of themselves as dignified people. Each of us must become a participant, giving to society as much as we receive, whether emotionally, physically, materially, or otherwise. In other words, a person's fundamental responsibility to others is inspirational, motivational, interpersonal, or intersubjective in terms of being with, giving hope, and evoking dignity. At bottom, every individual is seeking another person, whether in family, friends, or other relationship. Co-Being demands that each of us be a brother, our brother's keeper. Poverty probably exists in every society. Saying the ideal society should have no poverty might well be unrealistic. The state should cooperate with the private sector in lessening poverty, knowing well that we may never erase poverty from society. We should volunteer and pay taxes toward helping lessen poverty. People must continually monitor situations to determine if those in poverty are really poor, or if they are making an effort to escape poverty.

Taxes and money enter soon thereafter. The second duty I have toward the other is to help financially in a social context. When the other needs funds for a legitimate reason and I can help, my taxes go for those urgent needs. (I speak here primarily of taxes aside from police and fire protection, and other essential services, though even these services are irreducible to funds.) As Elliott Richardson[2] points out, being liberal is not the only option, because money will not solve all problems; but libertarianism is not a solution either. The proverb says, give a man a fish today, but teach him how to fish so he can catch his own food tomorrow. To be fair, liberalism has classical and modern aspects. Classical liberalism speaks about rights and property, while modern liberalism about human rights. Phenomenology and Richardson would reintroduce our duty to pay taxes into classical liberalism's concern for the individual's rights and property.

Taxes must be kept down, and all necessary taxation comes with strings attached. The money the state takes from me to help those in need ought to be given to the needy in terms of strict guidelines assuring the recipient that there is a message with this money. Every recipient must see that their future requires getting back on their feet, and not depending on this money. Phenomenologically, taxation is therefore a gestalt or whole that is more than the amount and kind of taxes. For intersubjectivity, if there seems to be a need for simply adding new taxes to previous taxes, then society has the duty to rethink its priorities, social conditions, and concepts of money and taxation. Determining taxation, like designing a product, is more than a technical problem. Just as a design (or production amount, cosmos, automation, computation) takes the individual's limits and capabilities into account, so taxation takes the recipient's dignity, and participatory needs into account.

Taxation is *ours*, which is to say it is the state that decides (along with my input?) I should give for another's appropriate needs. Thus, I give tax money not to a passive recipient, but to another person like myself. This amount and kind of money must take human dignity and self-government into account and manifest our attempting to disclose our social nature. The kind and amount are *ours*, in that they are not just dollars and cents external to our nature, or currency extracted from me and stuffed into the pockets of the recipient.

When taxation becomes a means toward solving any problem one imagines, or such fiscal issues as deficits and inflation, taxes, surtaxes, and the like present an ultimately serious issue. Reducing existence to money and to tax amounts and kinds brings taxes and money to the bring of mere objects for the spectator. If some taxation seems to solve the problem, then, like a narcotic, the state feels it beneficial to tax and spend more to solve the problem once it becomes bigger. As with Thurow's notion that computing is not always the answer, the sum total of taxation does not solve problems that are basically social in nature.

Where Lester C. Thurow[3] may object to just serially solving problems with computers on the assumption that solution does not constitute ethics, society does not advance by solving problems in serial fashion through taxation. Ironically, Thurow is a liberal and has sought considerable redistribution of wealth. The intersubjective approach insists that we begin asking if the issues apparently requiring more taxes actually ought to exist. Like the person who eats in order to solve an emotional problem, higher taxes only appear to be the answer. For Co-Being, if taxes are the answer to deficit, inflation, and so forth, and more taxes are said to do the trick for the future, where does taxation stop? Phenomenology means the necessity to rethink our habits, and nature instead of throwing money at problems.

Intersubjectivity, Co-Being, our taxes, requires preventing big government. Small government involves emphasis on the private sector, with individuals helping each other immediately, and not mediately through big government bureaucracy. Co-Being is nearer the lived world than is big government which taxes and spends without limit. The lived world is our immediate life world, not one reduced to the sum of objects around us. Intersubjectivity insists that government and taxes are primarily a social instead of a bureaucratic consideration. And the social factor in taxes means that what is good for society is less and less taxation, not more and more taxing and spending.

The social nature of people is nothing like socialism or pure egalitarianism as in John Rawls, where individuals are reduced to objects dependent on the state. Our nature as social beings means our abilities to think about what we are doing, the problems we seem to experience, and the best human ways of coming to grips with those issues as persons with dignity. Within the phenomenological framework for taxation, no person is only a source, and no person a passive recipient, of taxes. Socialism says persons are only a source and only passive recipients of taxes.

3. Excarnate Taxation: Social Versus Socialism

My phenomenology criticizes John Rawls's egalitarianism[4] and its manifestation in big government. For the egalitarian, the state must redistribute the wealth in order to be fair and just to all. Unfortunately, this type of thinker ignores the fact that some (many?) who receive tax money will not want to earn their own, and that many projects supposedly for public benefit are done only because the money is there.

Just as the learning process sees an extreme in terms of the passive student being stuffed with discreet facts, so socialism or egalitarianism tends to see individuals as simply having the right to money from others, as passive recipients of discreet dollars and cents. Here, the state no longer inspires and directs, but takes from the wealthy or other earner and gives to the needy or those perceived as needy.

Phenomenology can say that in Rawls, rights and responsibilities thereby would be separated. Wealthy persons have more a fundamental responsibility to give of their wealth than a basic right to this gain (though responsibility is more complex, as we have noted earlier). The needy have an almost infinite right to tax money. Thus, rights and duties seem not to intersect in the same persons, as in Co-Being.

The intersubjective criticism of socialism's call for more taxes emphasizes redistribution's or egalitarianism's view that existence is almost always a series of problems, solvable through cash. Presumably, the state never pauses to rethink social issues and their interpersonal, existential, intersubjective contexts. The government sees people saying they are in need and strives in the name of justice and fairness to take from the worker's earnings to merely convey money to the recipient. Where Husserl has indicated that the other is someone like me, liberals and extreme egalitarians argue that there are only the wealthy with money and the responsibility to redistribute this money to those without money and the right to receive. If the other is someone like me, they have rights and duties not just the rich and poor.

A technician designing a product simply as a technical problem assumes that the design is just to have dials, levers, knobs, and so forth, and the user is reduced to arms, legs, eyes, and ears as such. The strictly egalitarian state may often begin by developing federal programs for taking and allocating taxes, without assuming that someone like me is a person requiring personal, emotional, intersubjective appreciation more than just money. Since the state is not a monolith, it is possible that some people in the government honestly care and want to respect me as a person. They will make an effort to treat persons as persons rather than numbers or objects. However, the most general characteristic of an egalitarian state may well be its impersonal nature.

Once the state builds the program and bureaucracy, it can assume that persons are either rich or needy, and that the state need only give money to solve difficulties. Thus, the state generally tends to see individuals as those who have money and others who need it: there is no assumption that each person, regardless of funds, is fundamentally someone like me. Government officials are therefore only technicians believing that the rich are responsible for giving taxes, and the poor or any group with problems or need are automatically entitled to those (and more) taxes.

In this way, the egalitarian state in Rawls seems to be something external to citizens. Problems are external, existence consists of problems and difficulties, money in terms of taxes can be the primary solution, and the more problems there seem to be, the more taxes need to be raised. This redistributive view reduces the design of government and taxes to a purely technical issue and disregards the social and psychological nature of problems. Some issues call for taxes. But the purely technical, egalitarian state sees persons not as Co-Being, but as sources or recipients of funds. The technical way of designing taxes means hitting those with money in order to extract more from them, and conveying more of this to the needy. The needy exist. They require food, clothing, shelter, and money. We must help them primarily through the private, but also public, sector. Beyond these material things, the needy require being taught to help themselves so that they can get off an egalitarian state's programs for the poor. An egalitarian state is therefore overwhelmingly person-unfriendly. To be person-friendly, the state must acknowledge the other individual as someone like myself and not reducible to a source of money for the passive recipient.

If individuals become accustomed to receiving funds, they in effect can develop into tax-receiving addicts, believing money is going to be their hope for the future. A state then grows into a Big Brother instead of remaining as an inspiration to a brotherhood. Each citizen is an object passively observing the big, strong, mechanically working state providing a flow of money. The centralized state is external, an object, only taking money from earners and stuffing it into the recipient's open hands. Citizens share almost nothing in common; certainly the idea of Co-Being appears absent. Thinkers and others will describe people only as the wealthy and poor, not as Co-Being. In other words, the centralized state philosophy, socialism, for the most part, considers individuals in terms of their economic instead of intersubjective nature. Persons are only in light of their money or lack thereof, not in terms of their relationships, emotional state, self-esteem, or being with others.

Where intersubjectivity is the foundation of a social and limiting theory of taxation, putting people's self-governing capacity and dignity above money, socialism's notion of unlimited taxation looks at government officials as technicians manipulating money and people. The danger in reducing people and existence to problems, and problems to money solutions, is that the future merely perpetuates an addict's dependence upon tax funds. Citizens see themselves as perpetually, essentially in need of money, just as the pedant sees himself or herself or herself as the perceiver of data. Where the accumulation of data cannot provide a framework for understanding the data, so more and more taxes and a Big Brother government is unable to constitute a perspective for social and psychological satisfaction.

Redistribution of wealth stifles growth, dignity, and an open future by being a band-aid approach to difficulties. Imposing taxes without thinking about the consequences on the haves and have-nots assumes that people are only rich or poor materially. More crucially, this technique is indifferent to economic and social well-being. Paying out more in taxes prevents investments, money in circulation, and human development. Increasing taxation assumes money is the sum of discreet objects of currency, instead of a whole wherein we should neither inflate nor deflate. Phenomenology sees taxes, as an expression of human nature and not something to increase as the state sees fit. Impose taxes on those who have money, and they will go slow in purchasing, perhaps stop buying. This costs jobs.

Such imposition also demoralizes the ambitious to no longer seek self-improvement and career advances including more pay. Why work, the phenomenologist would ask, if we work for the government, instead of our rights and duties, including our duty to help others see their Co-Being? The tax on luxury items, for example, did discourage the wealthy from buying boats, jewelry, and so forth. Middle class workers making these items found themselves out of work. Additionally, what does this taxation do to the potentially rich? Does someone with the idea of getting ahead in the future realize that having the money will not mean being able to spend a reasonable amount on a luxury item? In that case, a prospective millionaire may lose interest in achieving major financial goals, when purchasing power can be cut through unfortunate taxation.

"Getting ahead" appears to be an American instead of a phenomenological view. Phenomenologically, we must reintroduce "getting ahead" into "remaining human and equal." This avoids two distortions. Phenomenology rejects "merely getting ahead by making money and ignoring the public good." The wealthy who earn so much by abusing their workers are getting ahead in the purely objective, positivist sense of being excarnate from the social. They do not care for workers. Even the compassionate boss who declines to share a portion of his or her fortune with the public is ultimately not socially desirable. Unfortunately, some Americans may get ahead in this fashion.

Phenomenology also would reject only remaining equal with everyone, and never trying to earn great wealth. For the phenomenologist, we must attempt to earn as much money legitimately as possible, and then share some of this with the public. Contributing to charity, donating to various public institutions, volunteering, and so forth, mean that the very wealthy can get ahead, and give back some of this money for the general good. Phenomenology is neither a vow of poverty nor selfishness.

More generally, higher taxes mean less buying power for anyone with money. Raising taxes thereby results in slower than reasonable economic growth, and could lead to recession. Increasing taxes is often seen as a way to solve deficits and inflation. Yet a centralized state sees first of all the issues of inflation and deficit as money problems, instead of as cultural decay. Tell people the state must take more from them in order to cut inflation or deficits, instead of rethinking government spending, and the general population then becomes a source of tax money instead of individuals capable of working and purchasing.

A serious dilemma facing egalitarians is what and how much to tax when taxation seems urgently needed. Does government tax gasoline? Food? What kind of food? Restaurants? Should the government establish sin taxes? What if we tax entertainment? Do we then proceed to define entertainment and see whether something is part entertainment? Implications of more and more taxation lead to reducing human activity to specific, atomized elements where departmentalization and overspecificity dehumanize life. To simply impose taxation on items often assumes that beings are not part of each other, but that bread is only bread, wine only wine. What of a food where bread and wine are mixed? This kind of delineation forces the seller and government to almost invent definitions and boundaries in nature that do not exist. Big Brother, once out of constraints, starts cutting up and objectifying existence and looks at individuals and their behavior as motions, substances, and techniques.

Alexander the Great cried when he learned there were no more lands to conquer. The liberal state seeks to control and conquer, not to inspire, cut taxes, and motivate. It believes people are objects instead of Co-Being. When it runs out of taxes, it increases current ones. When it finds no more things to tax, it cries and attempts to increase current taxes or find newer ways of taxing. This carries Cartesian dualism to the positivistic extreme, overclassifying things in the world within the false, artificial boundaries of monetary worth.

Such atomizing ignores the family, neighborhood, and personal responsibilities. Money is something coming from the external government, instead of being earned through honest work or being borrowed from our parents, or our bank. Commodification of commodities and money is perhaps the ultimate in dehumanizing society. Socialism distorts the social and therefore the personal and intersubjective.

However, poverty can also destroy initiative. People in poverty can lose hope and initiative if they find that public and private sectors are unwilling to help. Taxes are necessary for helping people escape poverty, such taxation must be tied to an general system of private and public effort toward enabling people to work their way out of poverty. Atomized taxation is akin to the pure object apart from subjectivity, no longer taxes for the person. This distorts the phenomenological idea of our taxes, since increasing the public funds for the sake of increasing them is excarnate from the social context.

In user-friendly design, anatomic research is not meant to prove the person is someone like us, but to help the individual, whom we basically assume is like us, to physically use a machine without getting hurt. The strictly egalitarian state designs a tax system not on the assumption that individuals are like us and once in a while need certain tax help, but that some are taxpayers who must pay more, and others are recipients who need more. Human Factors engineers who argue that machines are social and psychological and not just technical problems would clearly concur with the intersubjective view that taxation is a social and psychological issue as much as a technique of taxing and spending. Taxation is meant not to solve problems and create dependence on the state, but to help the needy with the message that this money is temporary. For some it would be longer if they are disabled and can never work.

Years ago, Chicago found federal money available and built the State Street Mall. With fewer people coming to the Mall, the city realized that it had done the wrong thing by turning State Street into a Mall. The city tore up the Mall and brought back State Street. Malls are useful only when there is a ready, captive neighborhood audience as part of the Mall. Suppose federal taxes were not available. State Street might still be there with no Mall problem to undo.

The deeper issue for phenomenology is not whether federal funds are available, but the nature of government and its design assumptions. A liberal starts with big government and believes that individuals who say they need money ought to receive virtually all they want. In egalitarianism, government is central, literally and politically, and the official's technical ability to develop big government justifies such size and scope. Helping citizens means providing money and not offering them the inspiration to turn to private enterprise as often as possible. Government officials dedicated to taxation as the answer ignore the private sector and the individual's ability, indeed need, for self-government and mutual assistance.

Co-Being points out that government does not deprive people of money in order to hurt them. Instead, by designing government such that it taxes and spends more, the official is turning away from a user-friendly to a technically possible government mechanism, and the people are hurt in the long term. Their future becomes totally dependent on Big Brother. Helping citizens means more than fiscal criteria. Intersubjectively oriented government lets individuals know the strengths, abilities, and potentials of private enterprise and personal dignity. Giving money because it is there can hurt in the long term for it robs the freedoms and dignity of the recipient. Yet if recipients are unable to work, tax money would be necessary for the duration of their disability.

If taxes are the answer, is there a limit, a constraint on the kinds and amounts? Co-Being, as user-friendly design, assumes that restraint is basic to human life: analysis or atomization ought to be strictly confined within the human context. Extreme egalitarianism sees almost no constraint on the funds it takes from the wealthy and gives to the needy. On this logic, the future holds almost an assured unilateral transfer of wealth from one group to another, thereby virtually causing a stigma: the rich only give, the poor only receive. That could result in the poor or other recipient (even cities and so forth) never trying to escape the cycle of nonparticipatory reception.

When does the egalitarian cease or slow down taxing and spending? Some may assume that a government program ought to begin, give out lots of money, then stop. However, many recipients will probably find a way to prove that such programs should virtually become integrated into the nation's life-style. Government intervention, perhaps never intrinsically wrong, can be more dangerous than not, in view of the potential for recipients to declare that without it, their lives simply cannot improve. The overweight person continues eating not for purposes of survival or nutrition, but for emotional stability. In the same way, the liberal has turned money into a drug, feeding the supposedly needy instead of intersubjectively showing them that dignity, freedom, the private sector, courage, and character, all carry as much importance for life as money.

Big government means mediate rather than immediate governing and help to the people. Money goes from the taxpayer to the bureaucracy, and then to the people: maybe. No role is left for the individuals, voluntarism, the private sector. Government is mere technique, the best way to get money from taxpayers, and then maybe the best way, mediately, to get to the people. But we recall that mediacy, however efficient, is nonetheless mediacy. True efficiency, true immediacy, is less government, not bigger government with more ostensibly efficient, but in reality merely mediate and therefore inefficient technique. Mediacy and efficiency are mutually inconsistent, contradictory. The more mediacy, the bigger the government, the less efficiency.

Just as cosmology is irreducible to the sum of natural laws, production amount irreducible to higher GDP, machine design more than technical solutions, automation irreducible to motions, computers to serial thinking, and the economy to quantification in service, so taxes are irreducible to kind and amount. Every tax must be *ours,* and not just the external funding; taxation must reflect human limits and needs and be conducive to citizens' dignity.

4. My Taxation: Subjectivism as Anarchism

If Co-Being criticizes egalitarians as overeager to see people as objects and taxation as simply external rather than *ours*, intersubjectivity similarly attacks the other extreme in government and taxation: Robert Nozick's anarchism.[5] These call for a subjectivistic view of taxes: my taxation or freedom. Calling for the minimal state, Nozick starts his work with the notion of individuals' rights instead of a phenomenological statement about reintroducing duty into rights. Phenomenology would have no argument with this, except that Nozick practices a different kind of dualism than does Rawls. Egalitarians argue that the wealthy have the duty to give to the needy, the needy the right to that tax money. An anarchist sees the opposite. Instead of saying that individuals have complex duties within the context of their rights, the anarchist maintains that an persons have the right to keep virtually all their earnings and earn as much as possible. Their responsibilities to the other, the needy, do not receive much attention, because it is the others who have the duty to do things for themselves: they should pick themselves up by their bootstraps.

Even anarchists cannot deny that one must give a helping hand when the other is in a desperate situation. Nozick sets the stage for arguing that well-off individuals primarily have the right to make money and retain as much as they can or want without the state imposing taxes on them. Like the educator calling for romanticism in learning without school, such as Ivan Illich,[6] the anarchist views individuals as capable of working and not needing tax money. The poor must meet their own financial needs. The state begins in anarchic and not reasonable, intersubjective terms. Phenomenology's view of the individual's social nature is clearly critical of this political subjectivism in anarchy.

If people are social or part of the natural and social world, they are inherently united with all individuals and exist in a given, prereflective state of society. The *Lebenswelt* or situations of lived history are due not to social contract, deliberative arrangements, or voluntary agreements. Phenomenology tells us the lived world is given to us and not something we decide to organize through our own efforts. Thus, the responsibility to help another in need is given, and not simply something I can decide. Each individual is both rights and responsibilities, and certainly not just one or the other.

Applied phenomenology maintains that individuals are born in a given social world not of their choosing. Additionally, they do not decide to leave a community to begin another one more to their liking. For phenomenology, the anarchist notion of choosing "my" community, "my" standards with virtually nothing imposed, "my" moral and related ideas, and certainly "my" taxation sounds very much like the subjectivism or my world against which Husserl argues. Taxes, society, and standards are ultimately *ours*, not external money as in egalitarianism, or my subjectivistic earnings.

Phenomenologists offer the social basis of attacking socialism (denial of individuality) and anarchist (denial of anarchy or state). For phenomenology, if taxation is irreducible to the external sum of dollars and cents, it is similarly ours and not the social contract contingent upon my ideas. Co-Being is criticizing anarchism or my subjectivistic thinking when it maintains that the world is ours, given, intersubjective, and therefore the context within which I find myself.

Whereas phenomenologists view the lived world as intersubjective, the libertarian implies that I am creator of my own standards and capable of developing my own community with others like me. The lived world is no social contract. Phenomenology might well argue that a social contract is perhaps a contradiction. Social means fundamentally Co-Being, unified, due to our nature and not my and your independent decisions. Basic to anarchism is the notion of my being no brother to my fellow person. It is the opposite of Big Brother too far from the center.

Intersubjectivity shows flaws in both egalitarianism's objectivism and anarchism's subjectivism. Whereas applied phenomenology or Co-Being look at humanity very seriously to determine the limited taxes to impose, egalitarianism seeks first to develop the centralized state to tax and spend or redistribute wealth, while anarchism begins with the individual's rights to earn and keep as much as possible and ignore the needy. I believe that applied phenomenology comes nearest to the moderate conservative in social, political, and tax philosophy. If egalitarianism believes in Big Brother and anarchism in no brother, social taxation argues for brotherhood or Co-Being. In a sense, egalitarianism sees the individual as an object juxtaposed to others throughout history, and anarchism's subjectivism considers the person as a mere subject virtually choosing the past, present, and future.

Phenomenological freedom does not mean we are basically alone, but that we can think and live as a free people unhindered from dictators, tyranny, and technology. Institutions are real, the contexts within which we live, work, and have our identities. Thus, phenomenological taxation allows participation, whereby individuals are so linked with others that each helps the other nonmaterially as a foundation for the monetary. In user-friendly design's rejection of emphasis on design at the expense of necessary training for the individual, we see the reasoning behind an individual-friendly design's rejection of overemphasizing the individual at the expense of necessary adaptation to and taxation for society. It is wrong to design something taxation to make it too easy for individuals to do as they please, too easy to retain their money and not pay to the government.

Where socialism makes it almost impossible to keep a reasonable share of *our* earnings just as unsafe design makes it virtually impossible to use a system safely, anarchism makes it virtually impossible for the state to take needed revenue from the anarchist. No system, in this case the state, can function without the individual paying required taxes.

Co-Being argues that existence is irreducible to problems (existence itself is not a problem, a probing, a question to answer). Existence and problems irreducible to money or taxes (intersubjectivity is social and not monetary even in a given, irreducible sense). Money and taxes are irreducible to dollars and cents (they are given, minimal, and not mere parts to increase). Financial problems (inflation, deficit as problem constituting reductive money as such) are irreducible to money and taxes. Financial problems are due to social life style, not to merely a sum of money or taxes.

Two wrongs (reducing money to sum in inflation or deficit, and then solving these with reductive taxation or money) do not make a right. Inflation and deficits are artificial, unnatural problems, caused by socially undesirable life styles. Any monetary solution is a band-aid approach.

Similarly, financial problems such as inflation and deficit are irreducible to the surtax: the summative tax means we have reduced taxes to the sum of money (legalized counterfeiting?), but surtax means the solution to a false financial problem is reducible to the sum of both the sum of taxes and of another sum of (sur) taxes. Thus, surtaxing becomes the sum of sums of parts. In other words, the payer stands back from given amounts and pays a sum, and in turn stands back from that sum to pay another sum juxtaposed to it. If atomistic taxes consist of juxtaposing dollars to dollars (violating the gestalt), then surtaxing is the juxtaposing of juxtaposition (original tax) to juxtaposition (surtax). That is, surtax stands back and observes the initial standing back. Where atomistic taxes implies that wrong makes a right, the surtax suggests that two wrongs make a right.

If atomistic spending and taxing could be unconstitutional, that may *ipso facto* negate the need, perhaps, of an amendment demanding a balanced budget on the federal level, or even line-item veto. Both the balanced budget and line item veto suggest that Congress first, serially decides something, and then the President may veto a line. Congress can first decide taxes in light of an amendment, and then the president can veto a line or the entire bill. Should certain things be primarily unconstitutional and the Supreme Court be there simultaneously with Congress and the President, generating the tax bills, atomistic spending and taxing is fundamentally unconstitutional and stops there, at the start, without need for further serial procedure.

Phenomenological cosmology on taxation rejects excarnate taxes, where taxation is reducible to the sum of money taken from payer and given to recipient. Intersubjectivity reintroduces taxation into embodiment, into the cultural context of people being with people, and helping the other to regain dignity. Co-Being reintroduces Rawls's centralization, redistribution, and egalitarianism into Nozick's notion of rights. We cannot excarnate Rawls and taxation from Nozick and embodiment. Both Rawls and Nozick are extremes; intersubjectivity is small government between big government as excarnate, and anarchy as no government.

The healthy nation must have a holistic attitude toward tax kinds and amount, and not raising taxes or having no taxation. Given our tendency to raise taxes each time something goes wrong and liberals believe higher taxes are the answer, it does not benefit a society that produces higher amounts of goods and services while making higher taxes mere routine and ultimately solving no problem. The healthy nation must have a holistic view of taxes; it may not have higher taxes for their own sake and argue that government is the answer and does more, or that taxes are the way to solve problems of inflation and debt when in fact the solution is life style, lower taxes, less government and balanced budgets.

It does no good for a nation to produce higher amounts of goods and services when it taxes people ever more and simply spends their money on the assumption that taxing and spending reduce problems. Taxes are taxes only *for* the people; people are *of* taxation. We must reintroduce excarnate taxation into social needs, America's Constitution.

EIGHT

PROCEDURE *FOR* SOCIAL GOAL

Cartesian dualism concerns the subject and object as discreet spatial locations, and phenomenology overcomes this by reintroducing object into subject as a whole. This is nonteleological phenomenology, because the objects are there, are going nowhere, and are involved in no procedure. I now turn to teleological or procedural phenomenology as it overcomes teleological dualism. This dualism means objects are a series of times leading to a final time distinct from the series. The final time is the goal or subjectivity.

Whereas Cartesian dualism considers subject and object as two different spaces, a dualistic approach to procedure looks at subject and object as two different times: subjectivity is the time of the goal, and objectivity is the sequence of times leading toward the goal. Just as phenomenology overcomes spatial or Cartesian dualism by reintroducing object into intersubjectivity, a procedural phenomenology overcomes time or procedural dualism by reintroducing chronology (*Historie*?) into intersubjectivity as goal. The object is the sequence of times whereby the goal unfolds. Goals and processes are not distinct.

Consider another example of overcoming Cartesian dualism. Gilbert Ryle rejects a university's buildings as a category distinct from the university. He argues that the university is the way the buildings are organized.[1] The buildings are objects going nowhere as such, and the university is basically another spatial concept. Interpreted procedurally, phenomenology substitutes procedure for buildings and the goal for university. Thus, the goal is just the way the procedure's times are organized. We do not first have the separate times leading to the goal, and then a final time during which the goal is realized. Applied phenomenology reintroduces procedural into goal.

This chapter deals with five procedural objectives: (1) a general theory of overcoming procedure-goal dualism, applied to; (2) study-test dualism; (3) organization-assembly dualism in product development; (4) campaign-election day dualism; and, (5) law-constitutionality dualism.

1. General Theory of Procedural Phenomenology

Where Descartes's thinking substance generates objects, procedural dualism denotes discreet or even interrelated moments of time, events, from beginning to concluding moment. Procedure's purpose is ostensibly to fulfill a goal.

Typically, procedure-goal dualism means that people start with a procedure's beginning moment, proceed toward the conclusion, and then at the final moment do the actual event where the goal is realized. In procedure-goal dualism, the goal is never part of the procedure, never evolves through or manifests itself in terms of the procedure's various times. Going through the procedures' times in no way influences the goal; the goal (*Geschichte*?) comes only after the procedure as a chronological succession of events (*Historie*?) has concluded, and then on a specific, final day or moment. The goal in procedure-goal dualism is sequentially distinct from the procedure leading to it. Seeing the procedure means sensing only the sequence or chronology devoid of goal, embodiment, direction, decisiveness, or meaning. Experiencing the procedure does not mean seeing the goal.

From the intersubjective perspective, the procedure in this dualism has been excarnated from the goal. A chronology of events is external to the goal in terms of being sequentially prior to the goal. Whereas Descartes's object is simultaneous, though unrelated, to the subject, procedure-goal dualism tells us the procedure as a beginning, middle, and conclusion of times comes first in time, and upon the conclusion, we see the goal.

To succeed in overcoming procedure-goal dualism, phenomenologists return procedure to the goal as an intersubjective event or context. Procedure and goal are fundamentally interrelated: beginning the procedure is ipso facto the start of the realization of the goal. Procedure and goal are temporally, chronologically, and sequentially simultaneous: seeing the procedure means sensing the goal evolving over time. Serial time is returned to a simultaneous procedure-goal unity. The end (as conclusion) is at the start; start and conclusion are not and cannot be two distinct concepts. Starting the procedure means beginning the goal's realization, and concluding the chronology is to conclude the goal. Phenomenologically, a goal is the goal of the procedure, the procedure only for the goal.

Additionally, the goal is intersubjectivity. The goal is our being, or Co-Being. Procedure is not just the external chronology, but is within intersubjectivity and *our* procedure. Social events mean people are interrelating with each other and therefore are engaging in an interpersonal rather than mechanical procedure or subjectivistic goal.

2. Overcoming Study-Test Dualism

Every student and teacher knows the meaning of the final exam. Students study during the course and take a final exam on the one day sequentially after the course of study. This dualism entails the instructor giving information to the student during periods of time called study, and the student then one day giving back answers on the test day. The day of exams determines if the pupil has learned anything. This suggests nothing has been learned or evaluated during study: evaluation occurs only on exam day.

Some instructors are enlightened. For them, the pupils can do various projects, perhaps take small tests all during the course of study, thereby gradually showing that they have been learning. These teachers do not divide the world into study and test. The study is the test evolving. We find no final exams, no one quantitative evaluation of the students. These teachers are doing it the phenomenological way, reintroducing study into test. To study is to be tested. To be tested is to have been doing something with the instructors over a period of time, not one day called test day. The study is ours (teacher and student's) instead of the teachers lecturing to the passive pupils. Put another way, study and test are not two distinct categories (as Ryle criticizes Descartes, the university buildings, and the university); study is only for the test, and the test is only the test of study.

Additionally, since studies or learning are, at least partly, to get a job and be placed in a career, we can overcome study-placement dualism. This involves denying that study and placement are two distinct times; it reintroduces placement (working, the job market, career, doing) into study or academic orientation as a whole. Academic work enables the students learn to put specialization and meetings or internships with potential employers into general learning or core curriculum. The relationship between core curriculum and the law, including constitutionality, becomes clearer and more intimate as the students learn that in learning general and special knowledge, much of this is part of the law of the land. We cannot learn knowledge without learning about the laws allowing knowledge to progress. We see this also in the last section of this chapter.

3. Overcoming Manufacturing-Assembly Dualism

In product development, the usual method has been for departments to operate serially in manufacturing products. Management makes a decision, gives it to purchasing, then engineering, then design, then finance, then marking, and finally assembly. This is serial management or organization. Some manufacturers, such as General Motors, have gone from serial to synchronous or simultaneous management or synchronous organization. Here, Preston G. Smith and Donald G. Reinertsen's Simultaneous Management Teams or SMTs consist of representatives from all departments, including assembly.[2]

Developing a product, for example, a car, means all individuals work together from the start. The beginning of the procedure to build a car means the start of the assembly, because assembly-line workers work with the other departments. The start of the development procedure is the beginning of the total assembly (goal). General Motors does not first have ideas developing through serially working departments, then come to the assembly. Assembly people are there with their input from the managerial beginnings. The company reintroduces organization into assembly as a whole. A car is made as *ours* (the entire organization's including assembly), not merely the auto idea given to assembly to put together. Product development is not a distinct procedure from assembly; development is for the assembly, and assembly is of the development.

4. Overcoming Campaign-Election Dualism

Some might suggest I use another term for campaign, perhaps elected official's term or other word more widely indicating a term in office than simply the time of campaign. My effort is to point out that the election ought to be simultaneous with a procedure or period of time during which leaders have started in office and come to the election day, or are hoping to enter office. We are familiar with the statement "the person has been campaigning for x-number of years.

Campaign-election dualism means our traditional procedure of electing leaders. First, the campaign begins with the candidates, then nominees, making promises, speaking around the country, indicating what they will do and what the opposition has done wrong. The campaign involves the masses only as listeners and poll answerers. As the campaign ends, the election day itself occurs, when voters enter the voting booth and then vote. Just as the final exam determines the student's grade, the vote on election day determines the leader. Except that the masses do not really vote for the leader; the electoral college does that.

Unfortunately, traditional campaigns mean the candidate need not have the right message. The campaigners need money, a good organization, perhaps name recognition (unless they are running against a very unpopular incumbent, in which case the people decide on an emotional basis against the incumbent regardless of who is the campaigner), contacts in powerful places, and reasonable physical attractiveness. The more unpopular the incumbent, the less the challenger needs in terms of effort. The campaigner need only dwell on what the public perceives as the nation's weaknesses, and can say a few things about getting the nation back on its feet. The unpopular incumbent, or a challenger with the right message, but none of the above material requisites such as money and organization, has no chance. For the most part, the traditional campaign involves telling the people what they want to hear, rather than what they need to hear.

Reintroducing campaigning into the election, the campaign procedure then becomes simultaneous with the election days. This simultaneity brings candidates and the people nearer to each other and forces a closer look at who should do what. Instead of putting all the eggs in one election day basket, an ongoing election would mean the election is not just like the much-criticized college-entrance that exams determine, through merely filling in of spaces on paper, the student's future.

The campaign-election dualism has meant that those running for office first promise, then are elected, then deliver. Typical elections suggest that the masses have power over the leaders. But Thomas R. Dye and Harmon L. Zeigler tell us that the election process is more symbolic than not.[3] A nation's masses are generally apathetic, ill-informed, and cannot really make policy decisions. Might reintroducing campaigning into elections imply that instead of the masses voting a person in or out, the people will only answer polls, thereby letting their level of satisfaction indicate their opinions, but not select a leader? Who would select the leader? If, as Dye and Zeigler believe, the elite are talented, informed, and ambitious and have the masses' best interests in mind, then these interests should be spelled out (to the extent that this is possible), and the leaders can come into office somewhat like corporation heads. Spelling out the nation's agenda and policy could well entail nothing less than a cosmos, a public policy or national well-being.

This is not to say that any corporate head may lead the nation. Bill Gates may or may not have our best interests in mind. Human Factors presents a good model for the elite. Experts who design user-friendly systems do not use opinion polls as guides to their goods and services. They do scientific research to discern the user's physical and social capabilities and limits. Elites who would run the country must be like these Human Factors engineers, taking account of the peoples' needs. These experts will perhaps never tell the people what the population wants to hear. Instead, ergonomics or Human Factors specialists would indicate what individuals should do and have.

The individuals best suited for this would be the elites, or, as Bell believes, the researchers and government leaders with the knowledge and insight, not necessarily computerized or quantitative. The elite would consist of members from manufacturing and information sectors. Members from manufacturing would protect their sectors interests. Election day proves little; campaigning proves the same thing. Both generate noise, but perhaps only satisfaction instead of national policy. With elections changed into town meetings ongoing discussions with leaders informed, capable elites can help determine who will hold office.

Which is correct: liberal (excarnate, big or mediate government), intersubjective (phenomenological, small or immediate government), or libertarian (subjectivism, anarchy, no government)? Applied intersubjectivity argues for the middle position. Elites might discuss this and indicate its merits to the masses, and thereby choose a leader. Traditional catch-as-catch-can methods of campaigning, dirty tricks and so forth, would be out. Campaign promises have no place in a procedure where the discussion could well be the ongoing legislative processes. Phenomenology might integrate campaigns and elections with the actual, day-to-day government processes where the elites, not masses, directly govern, legislate, and execute. Typically, the election system in every nation is excarnated from the governing system; incumbants take time off from their jobs to campaign. Yet, if the elite are given the total reins completely, governing and election processes become integrated and simultaneous.

Elections are imperfect procedures of picking office holders and are largely symbolic. The election cannot be reduced to one day that determines a nation's future. The role of elections must be thoroughly reexamined. Co-Being gives meaning to the more real system where elites lead or spell out what is to be, within the context of the masses' welfare and the nation's general health. One of the problems of our traditional system is that the unknown, untested, so-called outsider candidates, undoubtedly often arrogant and naive, can try to convince the masses that they are the right person because of their insights, dedication, and ability to bring about change. However do they have beneficial ideas? Do their philosophies help or hurt? People who do not know them have an impossible task, coupled with the fact that they are generally uninformed, and certainly not everyone will vote. Again, with money, organization, the right contacts, personal attractiveness, and so forth, and an unpopular incumbent or candidate against whom to run, the runner or challenger can win even with the wrong ideas, ideas that can destroy the nation. The traditional campaign is almost totally emotional, perception, and bias. Some people who vote know the right candidate, but most will vote their bias instead of what is right for the nation.

Can we educate the masses to make correct decisions for the nation? I do not think so. Most people do not care about politics, and would be unable to learn its complexities. Most schools cannot even teach the basics of learning. Special interest groups would vehemently protest such school teachings about political material running contrary to the groups' agenda. Many national security issues involve classified information that the masses should not know.

If, as in the United States and other countries, more than two candidates can run for office, who wins? A numbers game results. The masses or populace votes; the electoral college has the ultimate say. But if campaigning were returned to election as a whole, the elite themselves have the better notion of what policy is good, and can best put the right individual in office. In the end, some may argue that the best of three policies liberal, social (variously conservative, intersubjective), and libertarian depends on our assumptions and can be neither proven nor disproven. However, Co-Being wins if it means inspiring the people with small government and brotherhood, instead of either Big Brother taxing and spending, or letting people do only for themselves with no brother.

Within our system, giving the masses excessive control over the election process can lead to dangerous circumstances. The people usually blame the current leader for economic recession, and praise him for growth.[4] In simplest terms, that bluntly says the leader is either lucky or unlucky, and not competent or incompetent. If the election itself is not the final determinant of who gets in or out of office, and if the elite govern in an ongoing fashion, the elite can tell the people that economic cycles come and go, and often are shaky; that the masses should not worry about what is occurring. Elections should never be a tool with which the masses, even the electoral college, take out frustrations on an office holder who is not responsible for or has no control over the situation.

This is not to say that giving control to the elites is never dangerous. Excarnate elitism, rulers who are not concerned with people, can be equally dangerous. We must reintroduce the elite into the public, whereby the rulers take people into account. To recall the ergonomic model, Human Factors professionals research user capabilities and limits in order to design goods and services. These experts almost never design something, and then ask the general public if the person on the street likes it. In the relatively ideal society, the elite group respects every citizen. The elite do not need to cater to opinion polls and the like, as do or must politicians running for office and seeking votes. Elites should watch the people, not the polls. An ideal political system would not have polls. Elites are good when they acknowledge themselves as Co-Being, their being with the ruled.

Someone may ask how we rid ourselves of dangerous elites if not by voting them out. I respond by arguing that people may not know a dangerous elite person. We would hope the elite themselves recognize such individuals, and practice self-diligence. They would prevent dangerous persons from joining the elite, and remove such individuals once they discover them in their midst. For phenomenology, the campaign as objective series of times would be for the election, and the election only of the campaign. Campaign, and election cannot be two distinct times.

This sounds like paternalism, however it is democracy. The former Soviet Union was paternalistic. It prohibited private enterprise and freedom. My ideal government is democratic. The elite protect democracy. Who watches the elite? Members of the elite check and balance each other. If we do not trust the elite and need someone to watch them, government becomes complicated. Who watches the watchers? In a good elite, members watch each other. Our system of checks and balances is inadequate. Dividing government into three branches does not mean they check each other. If we need two or more branches, why not have two branches? Why not have four, five, or six branches? Members of a good elite check and balance each other because they do not need votes. Politicians cut deals and cater to voters for votes. Supreme Court justices are confirmed by politicians and decide which cases they will decide.

5. Overcoming Legislation-Constitutionality Dualism

In the previous section's spirit, seeing the campaign and governing procedures ought to mean seeing the election or decisions of the office holder. Campaign and election days must be simultaneous, the campaign unfolding the election. But the campaign and governing processes, if together, can mean something broadly important for laws.

Traditionally, legislatures make laws, and the executive implements them. We assume that the laws are not hurting the nation. However, one day someone challenges a law in the courts, and the law's constitutionality becomes the issue. Congress and the President can want a law, and the courts to decide it is unconstitutional. Is that logical or fair? Intersubjectivity tells us to reintroduce the legislative and executive procedures into constitutionality as a whole. Elites are consistent with Co-Being, if the rulers see themselves as Human Factors specialists sensitive to the ruled people. Elites become inconsistent when they become tyrannts, or, at the other extreme, so sensitive to people as to ignore what the nation needs. The ruling elite are the Human Factors professionals designing government, law, and the like, for the people as users. These elite see themselves as Co-Being, as one with the people in terms of wanting what is best for the nation.

As with simultaneous organization in product development, or simultaneous election, simultaneous constitutionality means that the conclusion of a constitutional decision ought to be present at the start of a law's debate and enactment. Constitutionality is illogical as it now stands: a law is passed, and then, sometime in the future, the courts come in (like the assembly worker, the student on final exam day, or the voter on election day) to decide if the law is legal, constitutional. Constitutionality should be simultaneous, begun with the legislative procedures. The present system is serial rather than simultaneous. Congress legislates (with presidential accompaniment), and the Supreme Court at a later date decides constitutionality. That is illogical. A Supreme Court as we have it is unnecessary. Constitutionality as an issue must be there at the beginning of legislation to determine what law is right, constitutional, legal. We need not have a Supreme Court to decide cases brought before it involving behavioral, criminal, or other nonlegislative matters. A Congressional or legislative cabinet department with far fewer than the present hundreds of members can make laws that are in fact constitutional they constitute human nature. The nation must have an agenda, and all cabinet departments including a legislative one (unless legislators are integrated within each department) would work simultaneously to develop laws.

In making laws, are we not assuming that the law is legal? Are we not doing something because society believes the law is legitimate and within the Constitution? If not, then there is a legislation-constitutionality dualism. Legislating should be the unfolding of a constitutional law, or a law's constitutionality. Legislation and execution cannot be distinct times from the time of constitutional decision. Instead, legislation (and execution) is only *for* constitutionality, and constitutionality is only *of* the legislation.

The Supreme Court has to be included in the legislative and executive procedure, determining if the law, in fact, is legal or constitutional as it is passed and signed. Phenomenology would combine the Supreme Court with Congress as the decision-making Cabinet Department. Put another way, the constitution as the law of the land sounds much like Bell's Coda for a (service) economy, or the enduring principles making up a core curriculum underlying all specialization and behavior. Our present system of making laws and then deciding their constitutionality at our leisure sounds reductive: we first spot parts and then build wholes. In legal terms we first pass bills and then consider their constitutionality.

Consider what the Constitution suggests. The Constitution is the legal document holding a nation together. The Constitution comprises the legal order or cosmos within whose context particular laws and specialization is spawned. Thus, a government ought to begin with the Supreme Court and constitutional order, therein asking legislators and the executive to determine which laws to generate within this constitutional whole. Once a law is passed and signed, one should not have to worry about its constitutionality. Constitutionality does not mean irreversibility. If the elite make a mistake, they would reverse the law. They would review laws periodically. If they learn that a law is incorrect after having passed it, they are not prohibited from changing it. Someone may suggest that we have too many laws to review. Perhaps we do not need so many laws at any given time.

Constitutionality as a concern must exist from the start. Seeing a law being generated, passed, and signed should mean sensing its constitutionality. If, during the procedure, the justices feel something is unconstitutional about the legislation, they would have the power to stop the procedure. The legislative and executive branches ought not to generate laws excarnate from the constitutional framework. Why should learned justices themselves not have the authority to suggest laws?

Recalling my first chapter concerning core curriculum, the fact that the law and constitution are intellectual things to know, all this becomes part of the student's core curriculum. If, as Benjamin Cardozo says, a Constitution means principles orienting our future[5] and not just applying to today's specifics, then, as Len Young Smith and Dale Roberson point out, a Constitution is not just part of our basic core, but its very nature: the core curriculum means the Constitution.[6]

6. Conclusion

Just as phenomenology, especially Ricoeur, reintroduces objectivity into subjectivity as a whole, so he would suggest reintroducing procedures into goals. As a result, applied Co-Being reintroduces study into test as a whole, product development into assembly as a whole, campaigns into election as a whole, and law-making into constitutionality as a whole.

Phenomenology, which is to say a phenomenological cosmology, rejects excarnate exams, campaigns, legislation and production. Co-Being reintroduces exams into study, campaigns into election, legislation and court decisions within constitutionality, and product manufacturing into the assembly line.

A healthy nation has a holistic view toward procedures of study and testing, campaigns within elections, legislations within constitutionality, and product development within assembly lines. A society does not benefit from higher amounts of goods and services when study and testing, manufacturing, campaign and elections, and, law and constitutionality are done in fragmented, serial organization instead of teleological phenomenology or simultaneous organization. Procedure is always procedure only *for* a goal; a goal is a goal only *of* the procedure.

NOTES

Introduction

1. Edmund Husserl, *Ideas Pertaining to a Pure Phenomenology and to a Phenomenological Philosophy. First Book. General Introduction to a Pure Phenomenology*, trans. Fred Kersten (The Hague: Martinus Nijhoff, 1973).

2. Edmund Husserl, *Cartesian Meditations*, trans. Dorian Cairns, 8th Impression (Dordrecht, Boston, London: Kluwer Academic Publishers, 1991).

3. *Ibid.*, p. 39.

4. Martin Heidegger, *Being and Time*, trans. John Macquarrie and Edward Robinson (New York: Harper and Row, 1962), p. 1.

5. *Ibid.*, p. 65.

6. *Ibid.*, p. 51.

7. Maurice Merleau-Ponty, *The Phenomenology of Perception*, trans. Colin Smith (London and New York: Routledge & Kegan Paul Ltd., 1962).

8. Paul Ricoeur, *Freedom and Nature: The Voluntary and the Involuntary*, trans. Erazím V. Kohák (Evanston, Ill.: Northwestern University Press, 1966).

9. *Ibid.*, p. 116.

ONE: Specialization *For* General Education

1. Judy Fauri, "An Alternative Career Option: The Teacher as a Training Specialist," *Action in Teacher Education*, 4:4 (1982), p. 5.

2. Alfred Schutz, *On Phenomenology and Social Relation: Selected Writings*, Ed. with an Introduction by Helmut B. Wagner (Chicago: University of Chicago Press, 1970), pp. 79-80.

3. Jerome Bert Weisner, in *The Challenge of Technology: Linking Business, Science, and the Humanities in Examining Management and Man in the Computer Age* (New York: National Industrial Conference Board, 1966), p. 10.

4. Arthur D. Hall, *A Methodology for Systems Engineering* (New York: D. Van Nostrand, 1966), ch. 8.

5. Nell P. Eurich, *Corporate Classrooms* (Princeton, N.J.: The Carnegie Foundation for the Advancement of Teaching, 1985), p. xiv.

6. See Richard Bellman, "Dynamic Programming, Intelligent Machines, and Self-Organizing Systems." Paper presented at the Symposium on Mathematical Theory of Automata, Polytechnic Institute of Brooklyn, New York, 24-26 April 1962, pp. 10-11. Also Albert Einstein, Address Before Study Body, California Institute of Technology, Pasadena, Cal., 2 June 1931.

7. Paul Ricoeur, *Freedom and Nature: The Voluntary and the Involuntary*, trans. Erazím V. Kohák (Evanston, Ill.: Northwestern University Press, 1966), p. 116.

TWO: Production *For* Community

1. Rodney Ferguson and Eugene Carlson, "The Boomdocks: Distant Communities Promise Good Homes But Produce Malaise," *The Wall Street Journal*, 72:9 (25 October 1991), p. 1.

2. Herman E. Daly and John B. Cobb, Jr., *For the Common Good* (Boston: Beacon Press, 1989), Part 2.

3. Paul Ricoeur, *Freedom and Nature: The Voluntary and the Involuntary*, trans. Erazím V. Kohák (Evanston, Ill.: Northwestern University Press, 1966), p. 128.

4. Ron Suskind, "Back to the Past: New England Banker, Sticking to Old Ways, Avoided Rivals' Woes," *The Wall Street Journal*, 72:88 (19 February 1991), p. 1.

THREE: Design *For* User

1. Edmund Husserl, *Cartesian Meditations: An Introduction to Phenomenology*, trans. by Dorian Cairns (Dordrecht, London, and Boston: Kluwer Academic Publishers, 1960), p. 111.

2. Alfred Schutz, *On Phenomenology and Social Relations*, ed. with an introduction by Helmut Wagner (Chicago: University of Chicago Press, 1970), p. 80. Also Alfred Schutz, *The Phenomenology of the Social World*, trans. by George Walsh and Frederick Lehnert, with an introduction by George Walsh, First Paperback Edition (Evanston, Ill.: Northwestern University Press, 1972), p. 159.

3. Richard A. Johnson, Freemont E. Kast, and James E. Rosenzweig, *The Theory and Management of Systems*, 2nd ed. (New York: McGraw-Hill, 1967), p. 388.

4. Barry F. Kantowitz and Robert D. Sorkin, *Human Factors* (New York: John Wiley & Sons, 1983), p. 14.

5. *Ibid.*

6. David Stewart and Algis Mickunas, *Exploring Phenomenology*, 2nd ed. (Athens, Ohio: Ohio University Press, 1989), p. 131.

7. Jack A. Adams, *Human Factors Engineering* (New York: Macmillan, 1989), p. 1.

FOUR: Automation *For* User

1. Alphonse Chapanis, "Human Engineering," in *Operations Research and Systems Engineering*, ed. Charles D. Flagle, William H. Huggins, and Robert H. Roy (Baltimore, Md.: The Johns Hopkins University Press, 1964), p. 539.

2. Barry E. Kantowitz and Robert D. Sorkin, *Human Factors* (New York: John Wiley & Sons, 1983), p. 10.

3. Jack A. Adams, *Human Factors Engineering* (New York: Macmillan, 1989), p. 354.

4. Shoshana Zuboff, *In the Age of the Smart Machine* (New York: Basic Books, 1984), p. 422.

5. Alfred Schutz, *On Phenomenology and Social Relations,* ed. with an Introduction by Helmut R. Wagner (Chicago: University of Chicago Press, 1970), p. 321.

6. Daniel Katz and Robert L. Kahn, *The Social Psychology of Organizations* (New York: John Wiley & Sons, 1996), p. 471

7. Adams, *Human Factors Engineering.*

8. *Ibid.*, p. 351

9. Kantowitz and Sorkin, *Human Factors*, p. 10.

FIVE: Computing *For* Society

1. Michael Heim, *Electric Language: A Philosophical Study of Word Processing* (New Haven and London: Yale University Press, 1987).

2. Paul Davies, *Superforce* (New York: Simon & Schuster, 1984), p. 103.

3. Joseph Weizenbaum, *Computer Power and Human Reason* (New York: W. H. Freeman, 1976), p.14.

4. Davies, *Superforce*, p. 243.

5. Jeremy Campbell, *The Improbable Machine* (New York: Simon & Schuster, 1989), p. 283.

6. *Ibid.*, p. 183.

7. *Ibid.*

8. Jerome S. Bruner, *Beyond the Information Given: Studies in the Psychology of Knowing,* selected, edited, and introduced by Jeremy M. Anglin (New York: W. W. Norton & Company, Inc., 1973), p. 397.

9. Heim, *Electric Language.*

10. Stuart E. Dreyfus and Hubert L. Dreyfus, "Making a Mind Versus Modeling the Brain," *Daedalus*, 117:1 (1988), pp. 24-25.

11. Algis Mickunas and David Stewart, *Exploring Phenomenology*, 2nd ed. (Athens, Ohio: Ohio University Press, 1989) p. 113.

SIX: Information *For* Manufacturing

1. Daniel Bell, *The Coming of Post-Industrial Society* (New York: Basic Books, 1983), pp. 14-43.

2. Lester C. Thurow, "A World Class Economy: Getting Back Into the Ring," *Technology Review* (August/September 1985), p. 29.

SEVEN: Taxation *For* Society

1. Paulo Freire, *Pedagogy of the Oppressed*, trans. Myra Bergman Ramos (New York: Continuum, 1992), ch. 2.

2. Elliott Richardson, *The Creative Balance* (New York: Basic Books, 1974), pp. 304-342.

3. Lester C. Thurow, *Generating Inequality* (New York: Basic Books, 1975), p. 54.

4. John Rawls, *A Theory of Justice* (Cambridge, Mass.: Harvard University Press, 1971).

5. Robert Nozick, *Anarchy, State, and Utopia* (New York: Basic Books, 1974).

6. Ivan Illich, *Deschooling Society* (New York: Harper & Row, 1972).

EIGHT: Procedure *For* Social Goal

1. Gilbert Ryle, *The Concept of Mind* (London and Chicago: University of Chicago Press, 1984), p. 16.

2. See Preston G. Smith and Donald G. Reinertsen, *Developing Products in Half the Time* (New York: Van Nostrand Reinhold, 1991); Steven E. Plumb, "It's Teamup Time at Buick Engineering," *Ward's Auto World* (March 1990); Gary S. Vasilash, "Another First at Flint," *Production* (March 1990); Robert Wrubel, "GM Finally Fights Back," *FW Magazine* (26 November 1991).

3. Thomas R. Dye and Harmon L. Zeigler, *The Irony of Democracy* (Monterey, Cal.: Brooks/Cole Publishing, 1984), p. 159.

4. *Ibid.*, p. 161.

5. Benjamin Cardozo, *The Nature of the Judicial Process* (New Haven, Conn.: Yale University Press, 1965), pp. 83-84.

6. Len Young Smith and Dale Roberson, *Business Law*, 3rd ed. (St. Paul, Minn.: West Publishing, 1971), p. 1.

BIBLIOGRAPHY

Adams, Jack A. *Human Factors Engineering*. New York: Macmillian, 1989.

Bellman, Richard. "Dynamic Programming, Intelligent Machines, and Self-Organizing Systems." Paper presented at the Symposium on Mathematical Theory of Automata, Polytechnic Institute of Brooklyn, New York, 24-26 April 1962.

Bruner, Jerome S. *Beyond the Information Given: Studies in the Psychology of Knowing*. selected, edited, and introduced by Jeremy M. Anglin, 2nd ed. New York: W. W. Norton & Company, Inc., 1973.

Campbell, Jeremy. *The Improbable Machine*. New York: Simon and Schuster, 1989.

Cardozo, Benjamin. *The Nature of the Judicial Process*. New Haven, Conn: Yale University Press, 1965.

Dreyfus, Stuart E. and Hubert L. Dreyfus. "Making a Mind Versus Modeling the Brain," *Daedalus*, 117:1, 1988.

Dye, Thomas R. and Harmon L. Zeigler. *The Irony of Democracy.* Monterey, Cal.: Brooks/ Cole Publishing, 1984.

Eurich, Nell P. *Corporate Classrooms.* Princeton, N.J.: The Carnegie Foundation for the Advancement of Teaching, 1985.

Freire, Paulo. *Pedagogy of the Oppressed.* Trans. Myra Bergman Ramos. New York: Continuum, 1992.

Heidegger, Martin. *Being and Time.* Trans. John Macquarrie and Edward Robinson. New York: Harper and Row, 1962.

Heim, Michael. *Electric Language*. New Haven and London: Yale University Press, 1987.

Husserl, Edmund. *Ideas Pertaining to a Pure Phenomenology and to a Phenomenological Philosophy.* Trans. Fred Kersten. The Hague: Martinus Nijhoff, 1982.

Illich, Ivan. *Deschooling Society.* New York: Harper & Row, 1972.

Johnson, Richard A., Freemont E. Kast, and James E. Rosenzweig. *The Theory and Management of Systems*. 2nd ed. New York: McGraw-Hill, 1967.

Kantowitz, Barry H. and Robert D. Sorkin. *Human Factors*. New York: John Wiley & Sons, 1983.

Merleau-Ponty, Maurice. *The Phenomenology of Perception*. Trans. Colin Smith. London and New York: Routledge & Kegan Paul Ltd., 1962.

Nozick, Robert. *Anarchy, State, and Utopia*. New York: Basic Books, 1974.

Plumb, Steven E. "It's Teamup Time at Buick Engineering," *Ward's Auto World*, March 1990.

Rawls, John. *A Theory of Justice*. Cambridge, Mass.: Harvard University Press, 1971.

Richardson, Eliot. *The Creative Balance*. New York: Basic Books, 1974.

Ricoeur, Paul. *Freedom and Nature: The Voluntary and the Involuntary*. Trans. Erazím V. Kohák, Evanston, Ill.: Northwestern University Press, 1966.

Ryle, Gilbert. *The Concept of Mind*. Chicago: University of Chicago Press, 1984.

Smith, Len Young and Dale Roberson. *Business Law*, 3rd ed. St. Paul, Minn.: West Publishing, 1971.

Smith, Preston G. and Donald G. Reinertsen. *Developing Products in Half the Time*. New York: Van Nostrand Reinhold, 1991.

Thurow, Lester C. *Generating Inequality*. New York: Basic Books, 1975.

———. "A World Class Economy: Getting Back into the Ring," *Technology Review*, August/September 1985.

Vasilash, Gary S. "Another First at Flint," *Production*, March 1990.

Weizenbaum, Joseph. *Computer Power and Human Reason*. New York and Oxford: W. H. Freeman and Company, 1976.

Wrubel, Robert. "GM Finally Fights Back," *FW Magazine*, 26 November 1991.

Zuboff, Shoshana. *In the Age of the Smart Machine*. New York: Basic Books, 1988.

ABOUT THE AUTHOR

Michael M. Kazanjian is with the Publications Department of DePaul University. He has taught philosophy of education at DePaul University and at North Park University, and is initiating a pilot project in education and work at Waubonsee Community College. Kazanjian has authored or coauthored twenty scholarly papers, presented three conference papers, and had a paper included in *U.S. House Hearings.* His articles have appeared in *Contemporary Philosophy, Thinking, Delta Epsilon Sigma Journal,* and *The Meaning of Life.* He is First Vice President of the University of Chicago-DePaul Chapter of Phi Delta Kappa, and belongs to the American Philosophical Association, Philosophy of Education Society, Association for Process Philosophy of Education, Society for Phenomenology and Existential Philosophy, and Association for Development of Philosophy Teaching.

INDEX

VIBS

The **Value Inquiry Book Series** is co-sponsored by:

American Maritain Association
American Society for Value Inquiry
Association for Personalist Studies
Association for Process Philosophy of Education
Center for East European Dialogue and Development, Rochester Institute of Technology
Centre for Cultural Research, Aarhus University
College of Education and Allied Professions, Bowling Green State University
Concerned Philosophers for Peace
Conference of Philosophical Societies
Instituto de Filosofía del Consejo Superior de Investigaciones Científicas
International Academy of Philosophy of the Principality of Liechtenstein
International Society for Universalism
Natural Law Society
Philosophical Society of Finland
Philosophy Born of Struggle Association
Philosophy Seminar, University of Mainz
R.S. Hartman Institute for Formal and Applied Axiology
Society for Iberian and Latin-American Thought
Society for the Philosophic Study of Genocide and the Holocaust
Society for the Philosophy of Sex and Love
Yves R. Simon Institute.

Titles Published

1. Noel Balzer, *The Human Being as a Logical Thinker.*

2. Archie J. Bahm, *Axiology: The Science of Values.*

3. H. P. P. (Hennie) Lötter, *Justice for an Unjust Society.*

4. H. G. Callaway, *Context for Meaning and Analysis: A Critical Study in the Philosophy of Language.*

5. Benjamin S. Llamzon, *A Humane Case for Moral Intuition.*

6. James R. Watson, *Between Auschwitz and Tradition: Postmodern Reflections on the Task of Thinking.* A volume in **Holocaust and Genocide Studies.**

7. Robert S. Hartman, *Freedom to Live: The Robert Hartman Story,* edited by Arthur R. Ellis. A volume in **Hartman Institute Axiology Studies.**

8. Archie J. Bahm, *Ethics: The Science of Oughtness.*

9. George David Miller, *An Idiosyncratic Ethics; Or, the Lauramachean Ethics.*

10. Joseph P. DeMarco, *A Coherence Theory in Ethics.*

11. Frank G. Forrest, *Valuemetrics: The Science of Personal and Professional Ethics.* A volume in **Hartman Institute Axiology Studies.**

12. William Gerber, *The Meaning of Life: Insights of the World's Great Thinkers.*

13. Richard T. Hull, Editor, *A Quarter Century of Value Inquiry: Presidential Addresses of the American Society for Value Inquiry.* A volume in **Histories and Addresses of Philosophical Societies.**

14. William Gerber, *Nuggets of Wisdom from Great Jewish Thinkers: From Biblical Times to the Present.*

15. Sidney Axinn, *The Logic of Hope: Extensions of Kant's View of Religion.*

16. Messay Kebede, *Meaning and Development.*

17. Amihud Gilead, *The Platonic Odyssey: A Philosophical-Literary Inquiry into the* Phaedo.

18. Necip Fikri Alican, *Mill's Principle of Utility: A Defense of John Stuart Mill's Notorious Proof.* A volume in **Universal Justice.**

19. Michael H. Mitias, Editor, *Philosophy and Architecture.*

20. Roger T. Simonds, *Rational Individualism: The Perennial Philosophy of Legal Interpretation.* A volume in **Natural Law Studies.**

21. William Pencak, *The Conflict of Law and Justice in the Icelandic Sagas.*

22. Samuel M. Natale and Brian M. Rothschild, Editors, *Values, Work, Education: The Meanings of Work.*

23. N. Georgopoulos and Michael Heim, Editors, *Being Human in the Ultimate: Studies in the Thought of John M. Anderson.*

24. Robert Wesson and Patricia A. Williams, Editors, *Evolution and Human Values.*

25. Wim J. van der Steen, *Facts, Values, and Methodology: A New Approach to Ethics.*

26. Avi Sagi and Daniel Statman, *Religion and Morality.*

27. Albert William Levi, *The High Road of Humanity: The Seven Ethical Ages of Western Man,* edited by Donald Phillip Verene and Molly Black Verene.

28. Samuel M. Natale and Brian M. Rothschild, Editors, *Work Values: Education, Organization, and Religious Concerns.*

29. Laurence F. Bove and Laura Duhan Kaplan, Editors, *From the Eye of the Storm: Regional Conflicts and the Philosophy of Peace.* A volume in **Philosophy of Peace.**

30. Robin Attfield, *Value, Obligation, and Meta-Ethics.*

31. William Gerber, *The Deepest Questions You Can Ask About God: As Answered by the World's Great Thinkers.*

32. Daniel Statman, *Moral Dilemmas.*

33. Rem B. Edwards, Editor, *Formal Axiology and Its Critics.* A volume in **Hartman Institute Axiology Studies.**

34. George David Miller and Conrad P. Pritscher, *On Education and Values: In Praise of Pariahs and Nomads.* A volume in **Philosophy of Education.**

35. Paul S. Penner, *Altruistic Behavior: An Inquiry into Motivation.*

36. Corbin Fowler, *Morality for Moderns.*

37. Giambattista Vico, *The Art of Rhetoric* (*Institutiones Oratoriae,* 1711-1741), from the definitive Latin text and notes, Italian commentary and introduction by Giuliano Crifò, translated and edited by Giorgio A. Pinton and Arthur W. Shippee. A volume in **Values in Italian Philosophy.**

38. W. H. Werkmeister, *Martin Heidegger on the Way,* edited by Richard T. Hull. A volume in **Werkmeister Studies.**

39. Phillip Stambovsky, *Myth and the Limits of Reason.*

40. Samantha Brennan, Tracy Isaacs, and Michael Milde, Editors, *A Question of Values: New Canadian Perspectives in Ethics and Political Philosophy.*

41. Peter A. Redpath, *Cartesian Nightmare: An Introduction to Transcendental Sophistry.* A volume in **Studies in the History of Western Philosophy.**

42. Clark Butler, *History as the Story of Freedom: Philosophy in Intercultural Context,* with Responses by sixteen scholars.

43. Dennis Rohatyn, *Philosophy History Sophistry.*

44. Leon Shaskolsky Sheleff, *Social Cohesion and Legal Coercion: A Critique of Weber, Durkheim, and Marx.* Afterword by Virginia Black.

45. Alan Soble, Editor, *Sex, Love, and Friendship: Studies of the Society for the Philosophy of Sex and Love, 1977-1992.* A volume in **Histories and Addresses of Philosophical Societies.**

46. Peter A. Redpath, *Wisdom's Odyssey: From Philosophy to Transcendental Sophistry.* A volume in **Studies in the History of Western Philosophy.**

47. Albert A. Anderson, *Universal Justice: A Dialectical Approach.* A volume in **Universal Justice.**

48. Pio Colonnello, *The Philosophy of José Gaos.* Translated from Italian by Peter Cocozzella. Edited by Myra Moss. Introduction by Giovanni Gullace. A volume in **Values in Italian Philosophy.**

49. Laura Duhan Kaplan and Laurence F. Bove, Editors, *Philosophical Perspectives on Power and Domination: Theories and Practices.* A volume in **Philosophy of Peace.**

50. Gregory F. Mellema, *Collective Responsibility.*

51. Josef Seifert, *What Is Life? The Originality, Irreducibility, and Value of Life.* A volume in **Central-European Value Studies.**

52. William Gerber, *Anatomy of What We Value Most.*

53. Armando Molina, *Our Ways: Values and Character,* edited by Rem B. Edwards. A volume in **Hartman Institute Axiology Studies.**

54. Kathleen J. Wininger, *Nietzsche's Reclamation of Philosophy.* A volume in **Central-European Value Studies.**

55. Thomas Magnell, Editor, *Explorations of Value.*

56. HPP (Hennie) Lötter, *Injustice, Violence, and Peace: The Case of South Africa.* A volume in **Philosophy of Peace.**

57. Lennart Nordenfelt, *Talking About Health: A Philosophical Dialogue.* A volume in **Nordic Value Studies.**

58. Jon Mills and Janusz A. Polanowski, *The Ontology of Prejudice.* A volume in **Philosophy and Psychology.**

59. Leena Vilkka, *The Intrinsic Value of Nature.*

60. Palmer Talbutt, Jr., *Rough Dialectics: Sorokin's Philosophy of Value,* with Contributions by Lawrence T. Nichols and Pitirim A. Sorokin.

61. C. L. Sheng, *A Utilitarian General Theory of Value.*

62. George David Miller, *Negotiating Toward Truth: The Extinction of Teachers and Students.* Epilogue by Mark Roelof Eleveld. A volume in **Philosophy of Education.**

63. William Gerber, *Love, Poetry, and Immortality: Luminous Insights of the World's Great Thinkers.*

64. Dane R. Gordon, Editor, *Philosophy in Post-Communist Europe.* A volume in **Post-Communist European Thought.**

65. Dane R. Gordon and Józef Niżnik, Editors, *Criticism and Defense of Rationality in Contemporary Philosophy.* A volume in **Post-Communist European Thought.**

66. John R. Shook, *Pragmatism: An Annotated Bibliography, 1898-1940.* With Contributions by E. Paul Colella, Lesley Friedman, Frank X. Ryan, and Ignas K. Skrupskelis.

67. Lansana Keita, *The Human Project and the Temptations of Science.*

68. Michael M. Kazanjian, *Phenomenology and Education: Cosmology, Co-Being, and Core Curriculum.* A volume in **Philosophy of Education.**